Classic
FLORAL
DESIGNS

Classic
FLORAL
DESIGNS

Ed Smith

Sterling Publishing Co., Inc.
New York

Prolific Impressions Production Staff:
Editor in Chief: Mickey Baskett
Copy Editor: Phyllis Mueller
Graphics: Dianne Miller, Karen Turpin
Photography: Joel Tressler
Administration: Jim Baskett

Every effort has been made to insure that the information presented is accurate. Since we have no control over physical conditions, individual skills, or chosen tools and products, the publisher disclaims any liability for injuries, losses, untoward results, or any other damages which may result from the use of the information in this book. Thoroughly read the instructions for all products used to complete the projects in this book, paying particular attention to all cautions and warnings shown for that product to ensure their proper and safe use.

Library of Congress Cataloging-in-Publication Data
Smith, Ed, A.I.F.D.
  Classic floral designs / Ed Smith.
    p. cm.
  ISBN 1-4027-2441-1
1. Flower arrangement. I. Title.
  SB449.S547 2005
  745.92--dc22

2005008759

10 9 8 7 6 5 4 3 2 1

Published by Sterling Publishing Co., Inc.
387 Park Avenue South, New York, N.Y. 10016

© 2005 by Prolific Impressions, Inc.
Produced by Prolific Impressions, Inc.
160 South Candler St., Decatur, GA 30030

Distributed in Canada by Sterling Publishing
c/o Canadian Manda Group, 165 Dufferin Street
Toronto , Ontario, Canada M6K 3H6
Distributed in Great Britain by Chrysalis Books Group PLC,
The Chrysalis Building, Bramley Road, London W10 6SP, England
Distributed in Australia by Capricorn Link (Australia) Pty. Ltd.
P.O. Box 704, Windsor, NSW 2756 Australia

Printed in China
All rights reserved

For information about custom editions, special sales, premium and corporate purchases, please contact Sterling Special Sales Department at 800-805-5489 or specialsales@sterlingpub.com.

Sterling ISBN 1-4027-2441-1

Acknowledgements

I thank the following manufacturers for their generosity in supplying materials for this book.

For flowers and containers:
Melrose International, P.O. Box 3441, Quincy, IL 62305,
www.melroseintl.com

For pan melt glue and floral spray paints:
Floralife, Inc. 751 Thunderbolt Drive, Walterboro, SC 29488,
www.floralife.com

For Styrofoam® and containers:
FloraCraft, One Longfellow Place, Ludington, MI 49431,
www.floracraft.com

For glitter spray, clear sprays, and spray paint:
Krylon Products Group, Cleveland, OH 44115, www.krylon.com

For craft glues:
Beacon Adhesives Company, Inc., 125 South MacQuesten Parkway, Mount Vernon, NY 10550,
www.beaconadhesives.com

About the Author

Ed Smith

Design, especially floral design, is Ed Smith's longstanding passion. He is a graduate of Ball State University, earning a B.S. degree and a Master's degree in art education, and taught art in elementary and high schools. For several years, he owned a company that designed and manufactured handcrafted gifts and floral designs for the wholesale market.

Today Ed divides his time as a florist, artist, and project designer. Over 250 of his designs have been published in magazines, on web sites, and as project sheets. He is the author of *Making Classic Wreaths* (Sterling, 2004) and *Wall Flowers for All Seasons* (Grace Publications, 2003) and is working on a book about bridal flowers. Ed also was a major contributor to *Florals for All Seasons (Krause, 2002).*

Ed Smith is a member of the American Institute of Floral Designers and the Society of Craft Designers. Contact him via his website, www.edsmithdesigns.com.

Thank You

I love designing floral arrangements and designing for this book was a pleasure because of the generous support of manufacturers that supplied me with wonderful products — they're listed at left.

Every time I begin a floral design I imagine the recipients and how they will enjoy the finished arrangement. I feel truly blessed to create beautiful designs that others will enjoy. Thanks to my mother, family, and friends, who encouraged me in the making of this book. I hope you, too, will feel the excitement of creating your own beautiful designs.

Contents

For the Love of Flowers

I love flowers. Their colors, textures, and fragrances are a wonderful, exciting mystery. Designing floral arrangements has brought me great joy and has the added benefit of bringing joy to others. Each time I begin an arrangement I am excited about the mood the finished design will create. I have been making floral arrangements most of my life – hundreds of arrangements in all – some small and simple, others large and elaborate. Each arrangement has a unique personality, just like the designer who makes it. Often one arrangement inspires the next, and the cycle of creation continues.

In this book I'll show you how to make a wide variety of floral arrangements and teach you techniques that yield great results. Knowing the simple tips and tricks I will reveal will help you create professional, beautifully crafted arrangements. Many of the tips you will use over and over. I invite you to use the projects and supplies lists as guidelines rather than rules, and let the projects inspire you to make your own classic arrangements. Feel free to make substitutions and explore your own creative ideas as you work, letting your arrangements express your personality. Take your time and choose quality materials to ensure a long-lasting arrangement.

The excitement of choosing flowers, adding the design elements, and (finally) admiring the finished arrangement are all fun steps in the creative process of floral design. There are so many happy unexpected circumstances that can produce beautiful results.

I hope you have fun learning and designing. Let your materials guide you in creating arrangements you can be proud to say you made.

A Brief History of Flower Arranging in America

Colonial Period

Few accounts mention the use of cut flowers in America from 1620 to the middle of the 18th century. The Pilgrims brought seeds and roots of plants with them to America, but because of their religious beliefs they used flowers for medicinal – not decorative – purposes.

Later settlers made bouquets of flowers (they grew them from seeds they brought when they moved west) and native grasses and wildflowers. Their bouquets were similar to those of England and Europe of the time – sparse and restrained. Since there was little room for luxuries like vases on the ships that brought early settlers to the New World, they used pitchers, jars, and earthenware containers. Later settlers brought vases, urns, and epergnes that were popular in Holland and Great Britain.

Porcelain, glass, and silver containers began to be imported around 1700. Simple mass arrangements of garden flowers and dried materials, both symmetrical and asymmetrical, were arranged in the newly available containers. Mixed bouquets in bright and pastel colors in the tradition of Williamsburg predominated. Williamsburg arrangements, made with a variety of flowers grown in the gardens of Virginia, were fan-shaped bouquets with solid masses of blooms in the center and feathery grasses and flowers around the perimeter. Flowers were dried during the spring and summer for display in the winter. Gardens of the time grew lilies, roses, hollyhocks, sunflowers, violets, carnations, and Dutch bulbs of all kinds.

Victorian Era

The Victorian period in America reflected the tastes of England. Ornate containers of porcelain, silver, and bronze were stuffed to overflowing with flowers in mass arrangements that were structured and stiff. Cool colors, especially purple and dark blue, were very popular along with white. This also was the time of the fragrant, tight round bouquet called the tussie mussie. Flowers were assigned a meaning; for example, a red rose represented passion.

1910 to the Present

After the death of Queen Victoria, crowded, stiff arrangements began to be replaced with more natural forms and pastel

colors. Early in the 20th century containers made of etched glass, pottery, and French porcelain were decorated with natural flowers, birds, and butterflies. Small clusters of flowers – about as many as could be held in one hand – were placed in them. Flower stems were short (only as tall as the vase or shorter).

During this time Americans began to be aware of Japanese art of line arrangements. Branches of shrubs and trees were placed in low bowls to mimic Japanese design. When World War I ended, flower arranging became a more popular pastime in America; people used flowers from their gardens, and flowers from greenhouses were more widely available. Books about growing and arranging garden flowers were published.

The Garden Clubs of America came into existence, and their members developed formal techniques and an understanding of the elements and principles of design as it applied to flower arranging. Garden clubs were influential in developing styles of flower arranging. They trained instructors and shared ideas about design that acknowledged both European and Japanese influences.

Contemporary American style is a combination of traditional European mass arrangements and Oriental line designs. Today American floral arranging stresses elements and principles of design, use of natural plant forms, and (certainly) originality and free expression.

Gathering Your Tools & Supplies

Before you begin to make your floral designs you will need to gather some basic tools and supplies that make each step easy and help you achieve professional results. Most items are available in craft stores and stores that sell florist's supplies.

CUTTING & MEASURING TOOLS

Wire Cutters

Wire cutters are important when working with silk flowers – they are used in almost every design. It's a good idea to choose a well-constructed pair with easy-to-grip handles. A good pair can make your floral design projects a breeze, while an inferior pair will be painful for your hands. A spring in the handle makes cutting quick and easy; choose a pair that allows the blades to open wide enough to accommodate the stems of most silk flowers.

Bolt Cutters

Bolt cutters make it easy to cut heavy wire stems. Purchase them at hardware stores.

Pruning Shears

Pruning shears these are the perfect tool for cutting vines, branches, and twigs. You can cut natural materials with wire cutters, but pruning shears make a cleaner, smoother cut.

Knives

A good quality **knife** is a must for cutting natural stems, and a sharp knife makes cutting easier. Cut fresh stems at a 45-degree angle to allow them to draw water easily.

A **household knife with a serrated edge** works well for cutting and shaping foam. To make foam cutting easier and faster, run the knife blade across an old candle or a bar of soap.

Scissors

I recommend having **two pairs of scissors**: one for general cutting and one for ribbon. Use the general pair for cutting paper and ribbons with wire edges; use the other for plain edge ribbon and fabric. **Don't** use scissors for cutting wire – if you do, you will quickly dull and damage your scissors.

Awl

An **awl** – a sharp pointed tool similar to an ice pick – is useful for making holes in foam and artificial fruits and vegetables. Making a small hole in floral foam before inserting a large stem makes the insertion easier and keeps the foam from tearing and compacting.

Other Useful Tools

Tape measure or **ruler**, for measuring
Pencil, for marking
Small hammer, for help inserting floral U-pins
Gloves, to protect your hands

Pictured right: 1. Serrated edge knife 2. Wire cutters 3. Bolt cutters 4. General scissors 5. Awl 6. Pruning shears 7. Knife 8. Ribbon scissors 9. Tape measure 10. Pencil 11. Hammer

WIRE & ANCHORING SUPPLIES

Wired Wood Picks

Wood picks are small pointed wood sticks with an attached wire. They are used to lengthen stems, provide support, and bind items together. Picks make it easier to insert items such as a small cluster of flowers, ribbon loops, or bows into arrangements. The pick's sharp point gives a tight, twist-resistant insertion. Wood picks inserted in wet floral foam expand from the moisture and increase their holding power.

Wood picks come in a variety of sizes (common lengths are 2", 3", and 6") and colors (brown, natural, green). Items attached to a wood pick can be covered with floral tape for added security and to camouflage the wire.

Wood Skewers

Wood skewers are ideal for securing fresh or artificial fruits and vegetables into an arrangement – you simply insert the sharp end of the skewer into the item. Be sure to use natural wood skewers for fresh fruits and vegetables as dyed skewers will discolor the items and make them unfit for eating.

Hyacinth Stakes

Hyacinth stakes are green wooden sticks in various lengths (usually 12" or longer). They support stems and secure accessories in an arrangement. Hyacinth stakes are great to insert through several pieces of foam to help hold them in place inside a container.

Cable Ties

Cable ties are long, thin strips of plastic with a textured surface and a raised end. When the pointed end is placed through the raised end and pulled, it forms a tight, secure hold. They are commonly used to bundle electrical cords and cables but are wonderfully useful in floral crafting. They can securely hold stems, vines, and branches that would be difficult to secure with wire alone.

Cable ties are sold in many lengths and colors; black ones are specially made for outdoor use. They can be purchased at home improvement, hardware, and office supply stores.

Chenille Stems

Chenille stems (sometimes called pipe cleaners) are an easy, secure way to create hanging loops for wreaths. They are also useful for wrapping the ends of heavy stems before inserting them in foam – they help the stems grip the foam tightly.

Chenille stems come in a variety of colors; choose a color that blends into your arrangement (moss green and brown are great color choices for most arrangements). The soft fiber of the chenille stem helps it grip and prevents scratching of surfaces that regular floral wire might damage. Metallic and brightly colored chenille stems are fun to twist and curl as accents in arrangements.

Cloth-Covered Wire

Cloth-covered wire is thin wire tightly wrapped with thread. It is sold in several colors; green, brown, and white are the most useful for arrangements. The wire can be very fine to quite heavy. The thread covering allows you to tie knots, easily grip the wire, and hold items securely in place.

Floral Wire

Floral wire comes in many gauges (thicknesses) and is sold in straight lengths and as paddle wire. Heavy gauge wire (e.g., 16 gauge) would be used for strengthening heavy stems and providing support. Lighter gauge wire (e.g., 22) is great for wrapping the centers of bows and binding stems together. Floral wire on a paddle is useful for garlands and binding or securing items together.

Floral wire comes green and galvanized; green is used most often.

Floral U-Pins

Floral U-pins (sometimes called "greening pins") are U-shaped stiff wires used to secure materials like stems, moss, and ribbon in arrangements. Use them to secure moss over a base by inserting the pin over the moss. Secure a stem by placing it under a U-pin; insert a couple of pins at 45-degree angles in opposite directions for the best grip. U-pins are more secure if you dip them in glue before inserting them.

Anchor Pins

An **anchor pin** is a small plastic disc with a protruding plastic spike. Use anchor pins to secure floral foam in a container.

Other Types of Pins

Straight pins are useful for securing items like ribbon and leaves in an arrangement. **Corsage pins** and **boutonniere pins** have pearly ends. They are used to secure items and as decorative elements. Insert a corsage pin in the blooms of small flowers such as stephanotis for a decorative touch.

Stemming Machine - A stemming machine attaches a sharp metal pick to floral stems, allowing easier and more secure insertion of stems into floral foam, dry foam, or plastic foam (Styrofoam®). Picks are usually 1-3/4", 2-1/8" or 3" long. A stemming machine is an investment, and but it's a useful tool for those who want to produce quantities of floral arrangements.

Sandpaper

Use **sandpaper** to smooth and shape plastic foam and to smooth rough edges of wood and baskets that may have splinters. It also can be used to remove rust from wire.

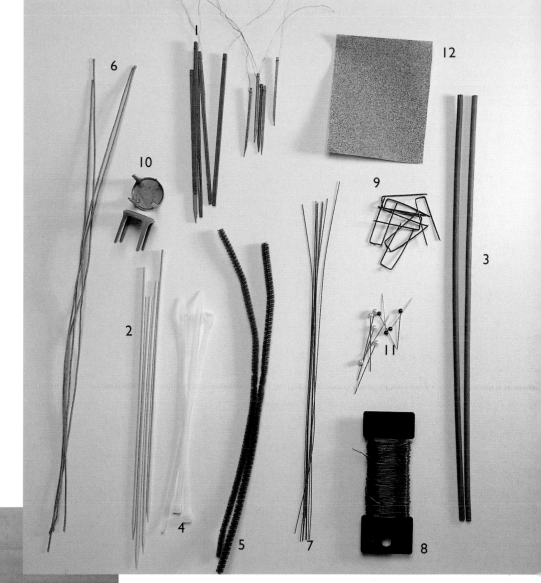

Pictured above: 1. Wired wood picks 2. Wood skewers 3. Hyacinth stakes 4. Cable ties 5. Chenille stems 6. Thread-covered wire 7. Straight floral wire 8. Floral wire on a paddle 9. Floral U-pins 10. Anchor pins 11. Pins (straight, corsage, boutonniere) 12. Sandpaper

Pictured at left: A stemming machine can be used for attaching a sharp metal pick to floral stems.

TAPES

Floral Tape

Floral tape is a self-sealing, colorfast, waterproof wrap that stretches to cover and camouflage wires, picks, and stems. Floral tape does not have an adhesive side; instead, it sticks to itself when stretched. The slightly sticky texture of the tape helps hold wires and other materials in place. It comes in a variety of colors and widths, including several shades of green, brown, black, and white. Choose a floral tape that blends with your design, such as brown on a natural twig or green on a stem.

Waterproof or Bowl Tape

Waterproof tape is a strong adhesive tape (green or clear) sold in widths of 1/2" and 1/4". It is placed across the top of the container to anchor the foam in the bowl, especially fresh floral foam. It is also called bowl tape.

Duct Tape

Duct tape, the cloth-backed adhesive tape, is sold in a wide variety of colors and widths. Use it to adhere foam to surfaces like glass and metal.

Pictured above: 1. Floral tape 2. Waterproof (bowl) tape 3. Duct tape

GLUES

Glue Guns & Glue Sticks

A **high temperature glue gun** can be used for most floral projects. It creates a strong, fast bond and is an easy way to glue silk flowers, dried materials, and novelty items into an arrangement. Use a **low temperature glue gun** on plastic foam (Styrofoam®) and other materials that are heat sensitive. Choose **glue sticks** that match the glue gun you are using.

TIP: Keep a bowl of cool water close at hand as you work with a glue gun. If you get hot glue on your hand, quickly dip your hand in the water to help prevent a burn.

Hot Melt Pan Glue

Hot melt pan glue is similar to glue stick glue. It comes in pellets and chunks and is melted in an electric pan to a creamy consistency. The advantage of pan melt glue is that you can easily dip items like stems in the glue and then insert them into your design. Pan melt glue is strong and flexible.

White Craft Glue

Heavy-bodied **white craft glue** is a great way to adhere some floral items. It dries more slowly than glue-gun glue so you have more time to adjust items before the glue sets up. It's great for covering a large surface, such as a vase with pot-pourri, and for leaves, ribbon trims, and dried flowers where glue-gun glue could leave a bumpy surface or a stain.

Floral Adhesives

Floral adhesives are sold in both tubes and bottles. They are used to secure fresh and silk blossoms and trims into corsages, headpieces, and intricate designs.

Floral Adhesive Clay

Floral adhesive clay is used to anchor plastic foam (Styrofoam®), pins, and accessories. It also can be used to secure candles in their holders. The clay comes in a roll 1" wide and is green or white. Adhesive clay will not work on the types of floral foam used for dried or fresh flowers.

Floral Stem Lock

Floral stem lock is an aerosol spray with an extended nozzle. Sprayed at the base of stems in an arrangement, it securely holds flowers in fresh or dry foam. It is fast drying and waterproof. Floral stem lock is often used to keep flowers secure in the bridal bouquets. Use caution and wear safety glasses when applying stem lock – it can splatter when sprayed.

All Purpose Adhesives

Clear-drying industrial strength glues (often labeled "all purpose adhesive") that come in tubes are useful for attaching heavier items and for gluing non-porous items like glass and metal. Follow manufacturer's instructions and cautions for use and drying times.

Pictured below: 1. Glue gun and glue sticks
2. White craft glue 3. Hot melt pan glue
4. Floral adhesive 5. Floral adhesive clay
6. Floral stem lock 7. All purpose adhesives

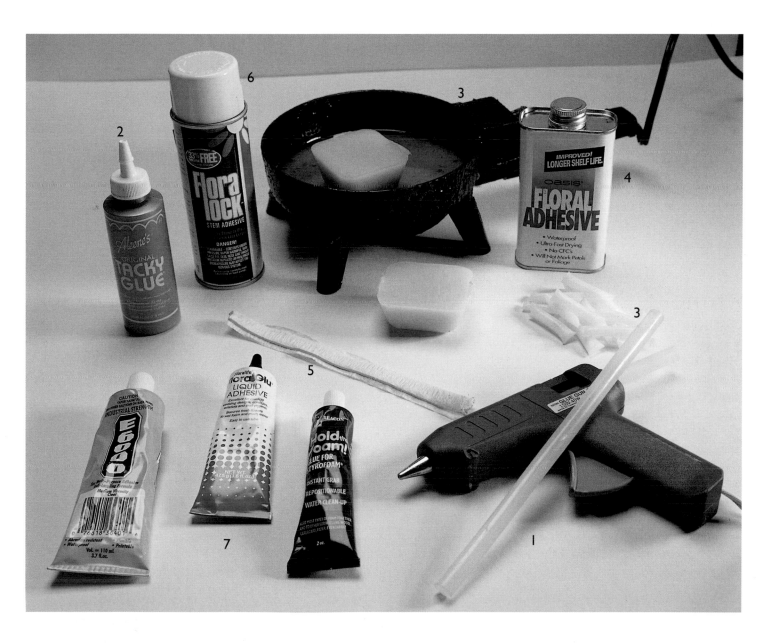

Choosing Your Flowers, Foliage & Accents

SILK FLOWERS

"Silk flowers" is the term used for almost all artificial flowers, whether the flowers are made of fabric, latex, paper, or (even) plastic. Quality silk flowers enhance your finished arrangements and make designing easier. Here are some guidelines for selecting silk flowers:

- **Details count.** Choose foliage and flowers with attention to detail. Look for veins, stamens, and subtle color variations. Flowers that are natural in color are always a good choice. Select an assortment of flowers with color variations for the most realistic look.

- **Wires help with shape.** Choose flowers that have wire inside the blossoms and leaves so that they can be shaped easily, and take the time to shape the flowers as you work. Starting at the base of the stem, shape the leaves and blossoms and bend the stems into gentle curves for a natural look.

- **Look for sturdy construction.** Quality silk flowers have securely attached blossoms. Open some blossoms and buds, if possible, to achieve different sizes and texture and to create visual interest.

- **Opt for variety in foliage.** Choose a variety of foliage varying the color, texture, and size. Foliage can create height, line, and texture in an arrangement and is often an arrangement's unifying element.

- **Prune.** Don't be afraid to prune foliage stems to remove some leaves for a more natural look.

- **Repair.** Frayed edges of silk flowers and leaves can be trimmed with scissors. Flowers with frayed edges can be held near a heat gun to seal the edges.

FRESH FLOWERS

Fresh flower arrangements are a delightful addition to any decor, and the beauty of fresh blossoms makes any day special. Although the arrangements in this book are made of silk and dried flowers, fresh flowers easily can be substituted in most designs, and the instructions for most projects work equally well for fresh and silk flowers. Although fresh arrangements don't last as long as silk or dried arrangements, the extra effort and in-the-moment quality make them wonderful works of art.

Choose blossoms in their prime or ones that are beginning to fully open. Here are some tips for using fresh flowers successfully in arrangements:

- **Prepare the flowers** by cutting the stems at an angle and placing them in water to which you've added a floral preservative. Be sure the flowers are well hydrated before arranging. (Allowing the flowers to stand in water for at least a few hours will help extend their beauty in the finished arrangement.)

- **Trim foliage.** Remove any foliage below the water line to prevent decay and rapid growth of bacteria.

- **Use the proper foam.** See the section on Foundation Materials for guidelines.

- **Insert stems deeply.** Insert your flowers deeply in the foam. Deep insertions keep the flowers secure and allow them to drink in more moisture.

FLOWER TYPES

Shopping for flowers can be overwhelming. Step into any floral supply or craft store and you will find hundreds of choices. To help you select flowers for arrangements, I have divided them into types that describe their general shape and appearance. Projects in the book suggest specific flowers, but you can substitute a similar flower in the same type (e.g., a line flower for another line flower).

Line Flowers

Line flowers grow in a linear shape. They help establish the height and width of arrangements and create movement and direction. Examples of line flowers include gladiolus, larkspur, snapdragon, delphinium, and liatris. Twigs, branches, grasses, and long slender leaves can be used as line flowers.

Form Flowers

Form flowers have distinctive shapes that are the same in each flower. Their distinct shapes make them ideal for the focal point in arrangements. It is often best to use an uneven number of blossoms (three, five, or seven rather than two or four). Examples of form flowers include tulip, iris, lily, bird of paradise, and calla lily.

Mass Flowers

Mass flowers have small clusters or a large number of blossoms at the end of a stem. Mass flowers are used to create both volume and the focal point in arrangements. Examples of mass flowers include hydrangeas, peonies, carnations, open roses, and large mums.

Filler Flowers

Filler flowers are multi-stemmed flowers that often have branching shapes. They add texture and depth to arrangements. Filler flowers include baby's breath, statice, wax flower, and small field flowers.

Pictured below, left to right: Mass, line, form, and filler flowers.

FOLIAGE

Foliage can be used for backgrounds, as filler, and to create contrast in arrangements. When choosing foliage, keep in mind the look you want to achieve. For example, are you creating texture? Adding height? Adding fullness?

Creating a background for the flowers? Adding visual interest? Beautiful foliage and berry sprays can unify a design for a polished, professional look.

Pictured above: Foliage and accents

ACCENT MATERIALS

Accent materials add depth and texture and create a mood in arrangements. Accent materials such as fruits, vegetables, pods, and shells can be used like mass and form flowers.

Artificial Fruit

MOSS

Moss is a wonderful natural addition to almost any design – it adds texture and color while creating a natural feeling. Mosses come both preserved and dried. Green sheet moss, Spanish moss, and reindeer moss can be used to hide elements like foam, picks, and glue in a design. Mosses can be used to cover a base before flowers are inserted, or glued on after the flowers are in place.

Soak sheet moss in water to make it more pliable and help restore some of its fresh green color. I often mix green acrylic paint with water to a very thin consistency in a spray bottle and spray it on sheet moss to recreate the look of fresh growing moss.

Sheet moss

Green-dyed Spanish moss

Reindeer moss

Natural Spanish moss

19

Containers & Foundations

CHOOSING A CONTAINER

Sometimes the container you choose is more important to the overall effect than the actual arrangement! The container sets the tone and mood for your finished arrangement.

Your first consideration is water – fresh flowers need a watertight container; silk ones don't. After that, be creative. Sometimes the perfect container is something you already own. Perhaps you have a pitcher with a chipped rim or an old silver teapot – both would be great for a casual arrangement, and both could hold water.

When using silk flowers, expand your search and your options. A drawer from an old sewing machine, an old hat box, or a terra cotta flower pot are just a few possibilities.

Here are some considerations for selecting a container.

Pictured above: Country containers

Placement

Where are you placing your arrangement? Be sure it will fit the space when the flowers are arranged. Is it narrow enough for the side table? Is it too tall to fit in the bookcase? Consider perspective. Where will the container be – above eye level on a tall shelf or on the floor and viewed from above?

Style

The container should work with the furnishings and style of the room where it will be displayed. It should look like it belongs.

Consider the style of your container. Is it contemporary, traditional, or country? *Contemporary* containers have clean lines and simple shapes. Glass, simple ceramic vases, and metal containers with little ornamentation work well in contemporary rooms. Contemporary containers are often large and dramatic. *Traditional* containers are refined. Silver serving pieces, brass compotes, cut and blown glass vases, and urns all fit the traditional style. Traditional containers have a timeless elegance. *Country* containers are durable, timeworn pieces. Natural materials like wicker, unglazed terra cotta, canning jars, and pottery are all great choices.

Shape

The shape of the container underscores the look and feel of the finished arrangement and defines the style of the arrangement. If the container has very strong lines, using those lines for the arrangement will create a cohesive look.

Height

The height of a container determines the height of the arrangement. A basic rule of thumb is that the height of the arrangement be one-and-one-half times the height of the container. For example, an arrangement in a 12" vase would be 18" tall, for a total height of 30".

However, visual weight is more important than actual height; arrangements that are open and airy can be taller, and ones that are full and compact can be shorter.

When using low, shallow containers the height depends on how visually balanced the arrangement looks. Tall arrangements in a low bowl will make the arrangement look like it might tip over. But adding visual weight to the arrangement will make the arrangement appear balanced.

Length

Containers for centerpieces (which should be low enough to see across easily) and other low arrangements should support the length as well as the height of the finished arrangement. A rule of thumb for centerpiece containers is that the arrangement can be one-and-one-half times the length of the container on each end. For example, a container 12" long could hold an arrangement that extends 18" from each end.

Pictured above: Contemporary containers

Pictured at left: Traditional containers

FOUNDATION MATERIALS

Almost all silk and many fresh floral arrangements start with one common denominator – a foundation. Knowing which one to choose makes designing easier, the arrangement structural sound, and the end product professional looking.

When choosing a foundation consider the types of flowers and materials you plan to use. (E.g., are the stems thick or delicate?) Projects in this book use a variety of foundations, allowing you to see the best uses for each type. Here are some examples.

Plastic Foam (Styrofoam®)

Plastic foam comes in both green and white and in sheets and in a wide variety of sizes and shapes like balls, cones, stars, and wreaths with straight and beveled edges. For most arrangements you will use sheets, balls, cones or egg shapes.

Plastic foam is lightweight and easy to cut and shape. It can be painted with acrylic paints or spray paints safe for plastic foam. (Use caution! Some paints and solvents dissolve plastic foam.) Plastic foam will not absorb water and can be used outdoors.

The firm cell structure of plastic foam tightly grips floral stems. Materials can be glued, attached with floral U-pins, or directly inserted in plastic foam. Plastic foam is not a good choice when working with delicate dried items unless the items are attached to wooden picks.

Pictured above: 1. Plastic foam (Styrofoam®) 2. Dried floral foam 3. Fresh floral foam 4. Spray foam 5. Marbles 6. River rocks 7. Branches 8. Acrylic water

Dried (Silk) Foam

Dried (silk) foam is sold in bricks and comes in brown, gray, and green colors. It is very lightweight, has a sand-like texture, and can be easily cut and shaped with a knife. Dried foam is ideal for delicate and soft-stemmed flowers and stems. Because it shatters if lots of heavy stems are inserted, it is not recommended for heavy arrangements.

Use glue, tape, or wire to anchor dried foam in containers; floral clay adhesive does not work.

Fresh Floral Foam

Fresh floral foam, which is used with fresh flowers, is sold in green and, recently, other colors. It is very lightweight and easy to cut with a knife.

Fresh floral foam should be soaked in water until it is fully hydrated. Fill a sink or deep container with water, add floral preservative, and place the foam in the water. Allow the foam to fully absorb the water. Do not hold it under the water (this could leave dry places in the foam). Fully hydrated foam will float slightly above the water. After the foam is fully soaked, cut to size with a knife.

Fresh foam is not suitable for use with silk or dried flowers. It can be anchored in containers with hot melt pan glue or waterproof tape.

Spray Foams

Foam sold in an aerosol container is becoming a more common floral foundation. It's great for delicate flowers. The foam is sprayed into a waterproof container, stems are inserted directly in the wet foam, and as the foam dries the stems are permanently fixed in place. Work quickly – you need to complete your design before the foam sets up. Some varieties expand slightly as they are sprayed.

Marbles, River Rocks & Pebbles

Marbles, river rock, pebbles, and other loose materials can be used to loosely hold floral stems. These materials add visual interest and weight to arrangements and are beautiful in clear glass containers.

Branches & Twigs

Soft, pliable branches and twigs can be inserted in containers to form a loose support for floral materials. In clear glass containers, they add visual interest and texture to arrangements. Using natural materials like twigs, branches, and stones is called *hana-kubari* in Ikebana floral design.

Acrylic Resin Water

Acrylic "water" is a clear resin that hardens to look like water in a container. The resin hold stems permanently in place.

PAINTS

Here are some paints, colorants, and sealers I use for floral designs.

Floral Spray Paints

Floral spray paints can lightly enhance flowers and accessories with translucent color. Use them to add a touch of color or easily alter the color of materials in a design. (I often use wood tone sprays to give a fresh look to faded baskets, pods, and grapevine wreaths or to tone down or antique colors that are a bit bright.)

They are safe for use on fresh, silk, and dried flowers, and can be used on plastic foam (Styrofoam®) (they won't dissolve the surface as some solvent-based paints do).

Sealers

Clear sprays in matte and gloss finishes can be sprayed on dried materials to keep them from shattering. Two thin coats (instead of one thick one) produce the best results. Placing the item(s) for spraying in a cardboard box will contain the overspray and make cleanup easy.

Special Effects Sprays

There are a variety of spray products for creating special effects, including glitter sprays, leaf shine, and stained glass and glass frosting sprays.

Acrylic Craft Paints

Acrylic craft paints can be used to paint containers, plastic

foam (Styrofoam®), and natural materials. They come in an almost endless variety of pre-mixed colors. Cleanup is easy – just use soap and water. Apply craft paints with a foam brush or artist's brush.

Waxed-Based Finishes

Wax-based finishes, which are sold in tubes or small jars, come in a variety of colors and metallic finishes. Rub them on floral materials for highlights and shine.

Basic Techniques

In this section are the basic techniques you need to know to make the arrangements in this book and to become successful at floral design. Learning the correct way to work with floral materials is important to the finished look and longevity of your arrangement.

Using Floral Tape to Lengthen a Stem

Choose a tape color that blends with the material, like brown on a twig, natural on wheat stems, or bright green on a fresh stem.

1. Working from the roll of tape unroll a small length. Place the end of the tape over the wire or stem to be covered.

2. Gently stretching the tape toward you, roll the tape diagonally, overlapping tape slightly to cover the wire. Stretching the tape in long, tight spirals will create a smooth covering. Tear the tape at the end of the wire and smooth the tape end around the wire.

Attaching a Wood Pick

Wood picks are added to stems to strengthen and lengthen them.

1. Hold the pick parallel to the stem, overlapping about 1". Twist the wire from the pick around the stem and the wood, working down the stem and the pick. Make sure the last couple of twists of the wire are below the stem and only on the pick.

2. Wrap the stem and pick with floral tape to conceal the wire and secure the pick to the stem.

Securing U-Pins

1. Place stem on foundation. Insert the floral U-pin at a 45 degree angle.
2. Add a second angled U-pin in the opposite direction for a tight grip.

Securing with a Cable Tie

You can use cable ties to attach florals to some types of containers or to hold bunches of florals together.

To attach florals to a basket or other container, place the stem against the surface and wrap the cable tie around the basket. Slip the end through the nub and pull to secure. Trim end of tie.

To secure a bunch of stems, place stems in a tight bunch. Wrap the cable tie around the stems, slip the end through the nub, and pull to secure. Trim end of tie.

Preparing Containers

Taking the time to prepare your container properly will result in a beautiful design that will last a long time. A properly prepared container is the foundation of your arrangement, and it needs to be strong and secure to support the finished design. In the excitement of beginning a floral design, don't make the mistake of not properly preparing the container. It many not seem that important, but it is one of the secrets to success.

In this section I show several ways to prepare containers. First, some rules:

1. **Make sure it's clean and dry.** Containers should be clean and dry before you prepare them.
2. **Choose the appropriate foundation.** Use plastic foam (Styrofoam®) for arrangements with heavy stems and many insertions, dried floral foam for arrangements that include dried and delicate stems, and fresh floral foam for arranging fresh flowers. Allow the foam to extend slightly above the opening of the container for easy horizontal insertions.
3. **Use a plastic liner**, such as a plastic food storage container or a plant saucer, in valuable containers or when you want to be able to remove the arrangement from the container.
4. **Secure and cover.** Make sure the foundation is securely anchored and covered. Remember floral adhesive clay will not adhere dry floral foam or fresh floral foam. CAUTIONS: Don't use floral adhesive clay or hot glue on silver containers – you can permanently damage the surface. Add weight (marbles, rocks, gravel, or sand) to tall or lightweight containers that could tip easily.

Using Spray Floral Foam

Spray foam is great for delicate flowers. As the foam dries, the stems are permanently fixed in place. With spray foam, you need to complete your design before the foam sets up. Some varieties of spray foam expand slightly as they are sprayed.

1. Spray the foam into a waterproof container.
2. Insert stems directly in the wet foam. Let dry.

Pictured at right: If you're using a container such as this terra cotta pot with spray foam, cover the hole first with a piece of duct tape.

Preparing a Container with Slanting Sides

1. Place the side of the container on top of the floral foam and make impression with a serrated knife.

2. Use the impression as a guide trim the foam at an angle to fit the container. Cut a little at a time, testing the fit.

3. Allow foam to extend about 1/2" above the opening of the container and trim with a knife. Glue the foam into bottom of container with hot glue. TIP: If the foam doesn't fill the container, glue scraps of foam around the edges to fill the empty spaces.

4. Cover the foam with moss or other material. Secure with U-pins.

Preparing Baskets

Baskets make wonderful containers for many floral arrangements. Their natural qualities enhance the look of flowers, foliage, and fruits.

1. Unless the basket is tightly woven, I line it first with plastic to keep any floral foam particles or bits of moss from sifting through the weave. (Photo 1)

2. Cut floral foam to fit the basket. Stack pieces to get the proper height, which should be 1/4" to 1/2" above the rim of the basket. Secure the layers to one another with glue and insert wood picks or wood skewers through all the layers to help keep the foam pieces together. (Photo 2)

3. Trim the picks or skewers flush with the top of the foam. (Photo 3)

Photo 1 - Lining the basket with plastic.

Photo 2 - Securing foam with wood skewer.

Photo 3 - Trimming the wood skewer.

Photo 4 - Forming a grid of wire across top of foam.

Photo 5 - Tucking in the plastic.

Photo 6 - Covering the foam with moss.

4. Lay a wood pick on the top center of the foam and secure with a floral U-pin. Because most baskets have open weaves, glue and floral clay adhesives do not work well for securing the foam – the adhesive will seep through. A grid of wire across the top of the foam provides a stable base for the arrangement. The wood pick helps keep the wire from cutting into the foam. (Photo 4)

5. Tuck the plastic in the basket around the foam. Cut a length of floral wire about twice as long as the opening of the basket. Thread one end of wire through the weave of the basket near the rim on the left side and twist the end to secure. Place wire over the center of the foam across the wood pick and through the basketweave on the right side. Twist the end of the wire tightly and trim. Repeat with a second wire at right angles to the first. (Photo 5)

6. Cover the foam and wire with moss. Secure the moss with floral U-pins. *Option:* On larger baskets, fill in around the sides of the basket with plain craft or tissue paper before placing the moss. (Photo 6)

Designer's Tips: BASKETS

• *Using cloth-covered wire or wire taped with floral tape allows you to grip the wire firmly and easily.*

• *On small baskets, secure foam by inserting U-pins through the weave of the basket and securing with glue.*

• *Faded baskets can look like new with a coat of glossy wood-tone spray. To prevent runs, use several light coats rather than a single heavy coat.*

• *Light color natural woven baskets can be dyed with ordinary household dyes – simply prepare the dye in a container large enough to hold the basket, dunk the basket in the dye solution, remove, and let dry.*

• *A misshapen basket can often be soaked in warm water overnight and reshaped. Allow to dry before using. CAUTION: Don't soak baskets with added ornaments or baskets that have a varnish or lacquer finish.*

Preparing Clear Containers

Clear containers can be prepared several ways, depending on the look you want. Here are three methods for a tall glass vase.

Method 1

For designs where the stems will be visible and need a little support in the bottom of the vase.

You'll need to cut a piece of foam or use a plastic foam (Styrofoam®) ball trimmed flat on one side. The foam piece should be slightly smaller than the opening of the vase and there should be enough room around the foam to add a filler material.

1. Place a piece of duct tape on the inside bottom of the vase. Insert a skewer in the top of the foam and cover the bottom of the foam with glue. Insert in the vase and center on

the bottom. Remove the skewer and allow the glue to dry.
2. Fill in around the foam with the material of your choice (e.g., pebbles

or moss). Seasonal materials like candy corn, dried orange slices, and dried beans are fun filler materials to use in clear vases.

Method 2

For designs where the vase will be filled with a filler material like glass chips, small seashells, or sand.

Choose a plastic foam (Styrofoam®) cone with a base smaller than the opening of the container. Fill the container about three-quarters full with filler material.

1. Insert the cone, pointed end down, in the vase. Twist the cone into the filler material so the material hides the sides of the cone. Cut off foam at top if necessary. Add more filler material as need to cover the cone. Check to see that all sides of the cone are covered.

2. Secure the cone at the opening of the vase with glue and waterproof tape. Cover the foam with a few silk leaves (I remove the plastic veins first) and hold them in place with floral U-pins.

Method 3

For large containers.

If you are using a larger vase, you can cut a piece of plastic foam to fit inside the vase to hold the floral stems. When using clear marbles as a filler, I like to wrap the foam in aluminum foil – the shiny foil reflects the marbles and hides the foam. When using other materials, you could paint the foam or cover it in a color closely related to the filler material.

1. Cut a piece of plastic foam (Styrofoam®) the length of the vase plus about 1". The foam should fit inside the vase with room on all sides for a filler material. Leave extra room if you are using a filler material like marbles or river rocks. Wrap the foam in aluminum foil.

2. Put glue on the bottom of the foam and place it, centered, in the bottom of the vase.

3. Fill in around the foam with filler material. Here, I'm using clear marbles.

Preparing Bubble Bowls

1. Cut a piece of plastic or floral foam small enough to fit through the opening of the bowl leaving space on all sides to fill in around the foam with marbles or other filler. The height of the foam should be about one-fourth of the height of the bowl. Remove the foam.
2. Place a strip of duct tape on the bottom of the bowl. (Photo 1) (This gives the glue a good surface to adhere the foam.) Put pan hot melt or white glue on the bottom of the foam. Insert a wood skewer into the foam and place centered in the bottom of the bowl. Remove the skewer and press the foam securely in place. Allow to dry.
3. Fill in around the foam with the material of your choice, such as seashells, marbles, potpourri, or pebbles. (Photo 2)

Photo 1

Preparing Large or Tall Containers

These methods can be used with smaller vases or opaque bubble bowls. **Always** add weight with gravel, sand, or marbles to tall or large containers to keep them from tipping.

Method 1

1. Measure the depth of the container. Cut the plastic or floral foam this length plus a couple of inches. Center the foam in the opening of the vase.
2. Cut additional pieces of foam to fill in around the centered piece of foam. (Photo 3) Pack the foam as tightly as possible. Add glue around the neck of the vase to secure the foam.
3. Trim foam, if needed, and cover with moss.

Photo 2

Photo 3

Photo 4

Photo 5

Method 2

1. Fill container with gravel or other material to add weight. Choose a plastic foam (Styrofoam®) cone with a base the same size or larger than the opening of the vase. The top of the cone should fit snugly in the neck of the container.
2. Insert the cone and trim (if needed) with the pointed end inside the vase. (Photo 4)
3. Secure with glue. Cover exposed part of cone with moss. (Photo 5)

Preparing Low or Shallow Containers

1. Cut a piece of foam a little smaller than the opening of the container that will extend about 1" above the opening.
2. Glue in place. Bevel the edges of the foam. Fill empty spaces with scraps of foam. Glue the scraps in place to keep the foam from shifting.
3. Cover the foam with moss.

Photo 6

Preparing Containers for Fresh Flowers

Use only foam that is intended for fresh flowers, and be sure the foam is thoroughly saturated before you begin arranging. Using a sharp knife, cut the stems of flowers and foliage at an angle before inserting in the foam. Insert the stems deeply in the foam to allow the flowers to take up water.

Tape Grid Method

A grid made from waterproof tape supports fresh flowers in the vase. Be sure the container is clean and dry before applying the tape. The tape grid can also be used for silk flowers and foliage.

1. Using waterproof tape, form a grid across the opening of the container. Press the ends firmly to the container. (Photo 6)
2. Wrap strips of waterproof tape around the opening of the vase over the ends of the tape that formed the grid.

Glue & Tape Method

Be sure the container is clean and dry.

1. Trim dry fresh floral foam to fit inside the container. It should extend slightly above the opening of the container and there should be space around the fresh foam for water.
2. Dip the trimmed foam in pan hot melt glue so that the bottom and about 1/2" of the sides of the foam are coated with glue. (Photo 7)
3. Place the foam, centered, in the container. Allow to dry.
4. Place the container with the foam inside in a deep container of water. Allow it to soak.
5. Add crossed strips of waterproof tape over the foam. *Option:* Cut the foam, soak it, and secure in the container with strips of tape. (Photo 8)

Photo 7

Photo 8

Elements of Design

A basic understanding of the elements of design – color, form, line, space, and texture – will help you make good choices as you create your arrangements. The design elements show you what types of flowers to use, what shapes work best for a particular space, and how to create a mood. Applying the elements of design will make the process of designing easier and the results professional looking.

COLOR

Color is often the starting point of a floral arrangement. You might decide you want a bright arrangement for the kitchen or a soft pastel design for the coffee table. Just about everyone has color preferences. Color is the design element that gets immediate attention and causes the strongest reactions.

Color Terms

The common color wheel has 12 spokes that comprise three groups of colors: primary, secondary, and tertiary.

Primary - The primary colors (red, yellow, and blue) are the colors from which all others are created.

Secondary - Secondary colors are orange, green, and violet. These colors are made by combining equal amounts of two primary colors. For example, yellow + blue = green; red + yellow = orange; red + blue = violet.

Tertiary - Tertiary colors combine one primary color with a secondary color, such as red orange or blue violet.

Neutrals - Neutrals are white, gray, and black. In floral design, green is often considered a neutral color because it is the color of foliage.

Value - Value is the lightness or darkness of a color.

Tint - A tint is a color + white.

Shade - A shade is a color + black.

Warm Colors - The warm colors are red, orange, yellow, and colors with these three colors in their mixture. Warm colors are associated with fire and sunlight and evoke a happy, energetic mood. Warm colors advance; they are easily seen and appear to project forward in an arrangement.

Cool Colors - The cool colors are green, blue, and violet. They are associated with water, sky, and trees and are considered calm and restful. Cool colors tend to recede in an arrangement.

Color Harmonies

There are endless color harmonies in floral design. Here are a few guidelines.

Monochromatic
Monochromatic arrangements are all one color (including all its tints and shades). This is an easy, pleasing color harmony that most people like.

Analogous
Analogous colors are adjacent on the color wheel and include one primary. Red, red orange and orange is an analogous color harmony. An autumn arrangement of burnt orange leaves and pumpkins is one example.

Monochromatic

Analagous

Complementary

Complementary

Complementary harmonies are opposites on the color wheel. This Christmas arrangement in red and green is one example; another would be a spring design of yellow forsythia and purple violets.

Color Considerations

• In an arrangement, have one dominant color and other colors subordinate. Try 65 percent of the dominant color, 25 percent of the secondary color, and 10 percent of an accent color.

• Think about where the finished design will be placed. In candlelight, blues and purples may seem to disappear and brighter colors look paler.

• To achieve the appearance of balance, use darker colors near the center and base of an arrangement and lighter colors near the edges.

• The color of the arrangement's container should relate to the flowers. Ideally, it should repeat a flower color.

• To make a mixed flower arrangement sparkle, add a bit of bright purple or bright green.

Colorful Facts

In the West, black is the color of funerals. In China, the color is white. In most Western countries and Japan, brides wear white. In other Asian cultures, the bride wears red.

Blue is the most popular color in the world.

The most commonly recognized color is red, followed by yellow and green. All cultures have names for black and white; Eskimos have 17 different words for white.

Continued on next page

Vertical

FORM

Form and shape are synonymous in floral arrangements. The design shapes referred to in this book are vertical, horizontal, round, fan, and triangle. Form also refers to the shape of individual flower types (line, mass, form, and filler).

LINE

Line is important in floral arrangement because it gives the eye a pathway to travel and gives structure to an arrangement. Lines are created with flowers and their stems and with branches and foliage. The five main types of line are vertical, horizontal, diagonal, curved, and zigzag. Each helps express a mood.

Vertical – Verticals are the strongest lines in an arrangement and often define formal designs. Vertical lines create height and suggest strength.

Horizontal – Horizontal lines create width and define stability. Horizontal lines are restful and peaceful.

Diagonal – Diagonal lines suggest movement and drama – but don't use too many diagonal lines in one arrangement. This will cause confusion and look busy.

Curving – Curving lines suggest soft movement and let the viewer's eye move easily.

Zigzag – Zigzag lines suggest dynamic energy and are a subtle part of many arrangements, e.g., the movement created between flower types.

SPACE

Space is the area surrounding a design as well as the area between flowers. Space can be both positive and negative.

Positive space is the area an arrangement occupies or the space that flowers and foliage occupy. An area of positive space is often the focal point.

Negative space is the area between flowers and empty areas. A design without some negative space will appear crowded and tight. Negative space generally increases on the perimeter of a design and decreases near the base. This helps create rhythm in an arrangement.

Horizontal

TEXTURE

Texture is the surface quality of the materials. Texture can be both physical (rough, smooth, soft) or visual (dull, shiny). Using a variety of textures in an arrangement increases visual interest. Using similar textures creates a sense of harmony.

Floral materials and containers with rough or matte surfaces appear casual, while those with smooth, shiny, or soft textures appear more formal. Texture can seem masculine (rough and coarse) or feminine (soft and velvety).

Texture is most important in monochromatic arrangements because of the lack of color contrast. Other color schemes appear more interesting with the addition of textures.

Texture is more important in arrangements that are viewed closely (like a centerpiece) and less important in arrangements seen from a distance (like an altar arrangement).

Curving

Principles of Design

Understanding design principles as they pertain to floral arrangements will make your decisions about placing flowers and foliage, selecting a container, and creating a mood easier. Proper use of the principles of design will make your finished arrangement a powerful visual statement.

Balance - Balance in a floral design can be both physical and visual. It refers to the arrangement's equilibrium and is created by the placement of flowers, foliage, and accent materials.

Physical balance refers to the actual weight of an arrangement. Physical balance keeps an arrangement stable. *Visual balance* is how the arrangement appears. It is the perception that the design is stable. Visually unbalanced arrangements can be disturbing, especially if they look like they might topple over. Materials that are dark or bright in color are heaver looking, while light colors and small materials are lighter looking. Heavy looking material should be arranged where visual weight is needed. It often creates the focal point.

In *symmetrical balance*, both sides of the design are identical on either side of a center line. Symmetrical balance is formal. *Asymmetrical balance* is when things are not the same on either side of an imaginary center line. Asymmetrical balance is informal. In arrangements, asymmetrical balance is created by varying colors, shapes, and sizes.

Emphasis - Many floral arrangements have an *area of emphasis* or a *focal area*. Emphasis is created through the placement of dominant materials or contrasts. Accessories also can be used to create emphasis.

Harmony - Harmony is achieved when all the components in an arrangement blend well. Harmony can be achieved with the use of similar materials, such as an arrangement composed entirely of tropical blossoms, or the same color, like an all-pink design.

Proportion - Proportion refers to the size relationships among flowers, foliage, and container. The height proportion of flowers to a container is generally one-and-one-half to two. A good rule for the proportion of floral materials is 65 percent small or light, 25 percent medium weight, color, or size, and 10 percent heavy, dark, or large.

Proportion of the finished design or scale refers to the relationship of the arrangement to its surroundings.

Rhythm - Rhythm refers to the flow of materials through color, line, form, texture, and space. Rhythm is often created with repetition and transition. *Repetition* is the repeated use of an element (e.g., a color or a flower). Lines, textures, and shapes that are repeated also create rhythm. An arrangement with vertical parallel lines would have repetition that creates rhythm.

The way items are arranged also can create rhythm. A round design where the stems radiate from a central point has rhythm.

Unity - Unity refers to the relationship of all the parts of the arrangement that – if done well – have a wholeness or single effect. A unified arrangement showcases the entire arrangement, not the individual parts.

Unity is often achieved by *proximity* – the close combinations of flowers and foliage. *Transition*, the gradual change from one part to another, also helps create a unified arrangement. *Blending* the elements is important to unity, but too much blending can be monotonous.

The Projects

This section shows you how to make a variety of floral arrangements. Each project includes a supplies list, step-by-step instructions, and photos. I've also included an estimate of the amount of time it takes to create the arrangement and the level of difficulty.

Make adjustments for your individual style by substituting other flowers, colors, and containers for the ones I specified. And have fun – there are no mistakes, only opportunities for a creative adventure.

In the supply list for each project, the number of flowers listed indicates the **number of stems** to purchase. Some stems may have multiple flowers on them.

LEGEND - TIME TO COMPLETE

About an hour

1 to 2 hours

2 to 3 hours

3 to 4 hours

Overnight

LEGEND - LEVEL OF DIFFICULTY

Easy (Little skill required – great for beginners; hard to mess up)

Moderate (Some skill required; a little more complicated)

Advanced (Requires more time and skill)

NOTE: If you're a beginner, don't be put off by "moderate" and "advanced" arrangements – just study the photos and follow the instructions.

Basic Shapes

Most floral arrangements are one of five basic shapes. Once you learn to make these arrangements, you can create an endless variety of floral designs. The following pages show you how to make the basic design shapes: round, fan, horizontal, vertical, and right triangle.

Round bouquets are classic. They can look traditional or contemporary. A round arrangement is a great choice when you want to display several different types of mass, form, and filler flowers. (Line flowers are more difficult to use in a round design.)

Round designs are beautiful from all sides because the flowers radiate from a central point. When inserting flowers in a round arrangement, all stems should point to the center of the base material. I often pretend that the arrangement is like the earth and all the stems point to the center of the earth. The overall shape is symmetrical, but the flowers can be placed at random within the shape.

Round arrangements are referred to by many names. The *nosegay* is a loosely structured round arrangement dating to the 14th century. Nosegays were fragrant bouquets that were used to mask odors because people bathed infrequently. The *Biedermier arrangement*, which is German in origin, dates from the mid-19th century. In this arrangement, the flowers appear in tight concentric circles. Each row is a different flower and color. *Colonial* is another type of round arrangement.

Fan arrangements are one-sided, radiating designs with a semi-circle shape. (This style also may be called a *triangular arrangement*.) The flowers in this shape are symmetrical and have a formal quality. The framework is established with line flowers and filled with more line flowers or mass, form, and filler flowers. Both sides of the arrangement have equal visual weight, and all the flower stems radiate from a central point.

Visual balance is important – darker or brighter flowers are usually near the center and lighter or smaller flowers are at the edges. Fan arrangements work well in a bookcase or on a mantel. Altar arrangements are often this shape.

Horizontal arrangements are most often used as centerpieces. This style has long, low lines that are parallel to the surface on which they sit. Horizontal arrangements can be symmetrical or asymmetrical. The shape is restful and appears very stable.

Horizontal arrangements are attractive from all angles. They are perfect for a coffee table, in the center of a dining table, or on a mantel. Line flowers establish the length and mass, form, and filler flowers as well as accent materials complete the arrangement.

Vertical arrangements have tall, towering lines. They often look as if they're growing in the garden, like vertical gladiolas in a terra cotta pot. Proportion of flowers to container is important. The standard is flowers should be one and one-half times the height of the container; extending the height adds drama.

Balance is important; often a focal point is used at the rim of the container for balance and interest. Flowers and foliage will usually extend only slightly over the edges of the container. Vertical arrangements work well on the floor or anywhere you want the look of natural growing flowers.

Right triangle arrangements are asymmetrical. Line flowers create the shape of the informal design, and mass, form, and filler flowers create the focal point.

Visual and physical balance create the harmony of a right triangle arrangement, with lighter and smaller flowers placed near the outside edges of the design and darker and larger flowers placed near the center. This style could be displayed on a book shelf, on the bathroom counter, or at one end of a sideboard.

Round Arrangement

Level of difficulty:

Time to complete:

Pictured above left to right: green hydrangea, white daisy-like flowers, white viburnum, gerbera daisies, pink filler blossoms, purple scabiosa.

SUPPLIES

Container:

Low ceramic pedestal vase,
    4" tall, 6" opening

Flowers:

10 pink miniature gerbera daisies
    (form)

8 white roses and buds (form)

7 purple scabiosa (form)

4 ivory sweet peas (filler)

5 white viburnum (mass)

Pink wildflower blossoms (filler)

Yellow statice (filler)

Pale green hydrangea (filler)

White daisy-like flowers (filler)

Other Supplies & Tools:

Glue gun and glue

Wire cutters

Knife

Floral U-pins

Floral foam base material
    (your choice)

Sheet moss

Instructions begin on next page.

INSTRUCTIONS

1. Trim foam base material with knife to fit inside the container, allowing the foam to extend slightly above the opening. (This allows easier horizontal insertions.) Secure foam to container.

2. Cover base material with sheet moss. Secure with U-pins.

3. Trim the stems of the viburnum to a height appropriate for the container. (photo 1) Insert the viburnum in a cluster, centered in the container, at a height of about 5". (photo 2) *The viburnum establish the round shape and create a background for the other flowers.* (photo 3)

4. Insert the gerbera daisies, equally spaced and following the round shape, to a height of about 6". (photo 4) *The gerberas reinforce the shape and add contrast of color and shape.*

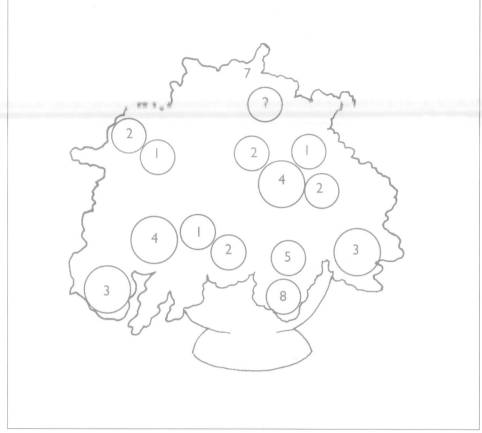

1. White viburnum 2. Pink miniature gerbera daisy 3. White rose
4. Purple scabiosa 5. Ivory sweet peas 6. Pink wildflower blossom
7. Yellow statice 8. Pale green hydrangea

Photo 1 - Trimming the viburnum.

Photo 2 - Inserting the viburnum.

Photo 3 - The round shape is established.

Photo 1 - Adding the gerbera daisies.

5. Insert the roses with the largest ones near the bottom. Add buds near the top. *This helps create visual weight.* Allow some of the roses to spill over the edge of the container.

6. Insert the scabiosa equally spaced into the arrangement as shown.

7. Fill in with sweet peas, pink blossoms, statice, white daisies, and hydrangea. *These add texture, contrast, and movement.* Be sure all the flowers stay loosely within the round shape. (photo 5) ❑

Photo 5 - Adding filler flowers.

Fan Arrangement

Level of difficulty:

Time to complete:

SUPPLIES

Container:

Pewter color ceramic urn,
   10" tall, 5-1/2" opening

Flowers:

3 white lilies with buds (form)

3 white stock (line)

2 white larkspur (line)

4 white roses and buds (form)

5 white lily of the valley (line)

Assorted white flowers (filler)

Other Supplies & Tools:

Sheet moss

Wire cutters

Floral U-pins

Glue gun and glue

Knife

Floral foam base material
   (your choice)

I. Lily with buds 2. Stock 3. Larkspur
4. Rose 5. Lily of the valley

Instructions begin on page 46.

INSTRUCTIONS

1. Trim foam with knife to fit inside the container, allowing the foam to extend slightly above the opening. (This allows easier horizontal insertions.) Secure foam to container.

2. Cover base material with sheet moss. Secure with floral U-pins.

3. Insert one stock to a height of 18" in the back center of the urn. (photo 1) *This establishes the height of the arrangement.*

4. Insert the other two stock to the right and left front sides of the container to a length of 9". (photo 2) *These two flowers establish the width of the arrangement.*

5. Insert larkspur to right and left of center stock to heights of 13". (photo 3) *These help define the fan shape.*

6. Insert stems of lily of the valley. (photo 4) *These help define the fan shape.*

7. Insert one lily in the center front of the container (photo 5) and another above and to the right and left. *The lilies establish the center of the fan shape.*

8. Fill in with roses, staying within the lines established by the stock and larkspur.

9. Fill as desired with white filler flowers. ❑

Photo 1 - Inserting stock for height.

Photo 2 - Inserting stock for width.

Photo 3 - Inserting larkspur.

Photo 4 - Inserting lily of the valley.

Photo 5 - Placing the first lily.

Horizontal Arrangement

Level of difficulty:

Time to complete:

SUPPLIES

Container:

Wicker basket, 3-1/2" tall, 6" square

Flowers, Foliage & Accents:

6 green apples (accent)

2 sunflowers and 2 buds (mass)

4 rust delphiniums (line)

5 gold ranunculus (mass)

7 red orange coneflowers (form)

6 orange berry stems (line)

3 pheasant feathers (line)

Autumn leaves (filler)

Other Supplies & Tools:

Awl

Wood picks

Floral U-pins

Glue gun and glue

Knife

Sheet moss

Wire cutters

Floral foam base material
   (your choice)

Instructions begin on page 50.

48

1. Green apple
2. Sunflower
3. Rust delphinium
4. Gold ranunculus
5. Red orange coneflower
6. Orange berry stem
7. Pheasant feather
8. Autumn leaf

INSTRUCTIONS

1. Trim foam base material with knife to fit inside the container, allowing the foam to extend slightly above the opening. (This allows easier horizontal insertions.) Glue in place.

2. Cover the base material with sheet moss. Secure with floral-U pins.

3. Insert two delphinium to the right side and two to the left to lengths of 14" and 11". (photo 1) Bend the stems of the delphinium downward. *These flowers establish the width.*

4. Using the awl, make a hole in each apple. (photo 2) Insert wood picks into apples (photo 3). Insert in the center and toward the left side of the basket. (photo 4) *The apples create contrast of shape and color and add visual weight.*

5. Insert sunflowers, one above the other, at the right front corner of the basket. (photo 5)

6. Tuck one bud to left of the sunflowers near the opening of the basket. Tuck the other one to the right of the apples.

Photo 1 - Inserting delphinium for length.

Photo 2 - Using an awl to make a hole in an apple.

Photo 3 - Pushing a pick into an apple.

Photo 4 - Apples placed.

7. Insert the ranunculus clustered behind the sunflowers.

8. Insert the coneflowers in a diagonal line from front left to back right to a height of about 6". *The coneflowers establish the height of the arrangement.*

9. Fill in around the delphinium with orange berry sprays.

10. Insert the feathers on the left. *The berries and feathers reinforce the horizontal line and add movement.*

11. Fill in with autumn leaves to add texture and to cover any exposed foam. ❏

Photo 5 - Fist sunflower added.

Vertical Arrangement

Level of difficulty:

Time to complete:

SUPPLIES

Container:
Terra cotta pot, 5" diameter

Flowers, Foliage & Accents:
3 blue delphiniums (line)
2 yellow lilies and buds (form)
Tallow berry stems (line)
Yellow statice (filler)
Bear grass (filler or line)

Other Supplies & Tools:
Sheet moss
Floral U pins
Wire cutters
Knife
Glue gun and glue
Floral foam base material of choice

INSTRUCTIONS

1. Trim foam base material with a knife so it fits snugly inside the pot and is level with the opening. Glue in place.

2. Cover with sheet moss. Secure with floral pins.

3. Insert delphiniums, centering them vertically, to heights of 18" and 20". (photo 1) *This establishes the height.*

Photo 1 - Inserting delphinium for height.

Photo 2 - Adding a lily.

4. Trim stems of lily and buds to about 4". Insert at the base of the delphiniums at the front of the pot. (photo 2) *This establishes visual weight.*

5. Insert tallow berries vertically behind the lily. *This creates contrast.*

6. Fill in around the flowers with yellow statice and bear grass. *These give movement and contrast.* ❏

Right Triangle Arrangement

Level of difficulty:

Time to complete:

SUPPLIES

Container:

Ceramic vase, 7" tall, 4" opening

Flowers, Foliage & Accents:

4 salmon color lilies with buds (form)

2 lotus pods (mass)

Red grapes (accent)

Orange berry stems (line)

4 long pointed (strobes) pine cones

White statice or filler flower of choice
    (filler Flower)

Other Supplies & Tools:

Sheet moss

Glue gun and glue

Wire cutters

Floral U-pins

Wood picks

Knife

Floral base material of choice

1. Salmon lilies with buds 2. Lotus pods 3. Red grapes
4. Orange berry stems 5. Strobes pine cones

Instructions begin on page 56.

INSTRUCTIONS

1. Trim foam with knife to fit level with opening of the vase. Glue in place.

2. Cover foam with moss. Secure with floral U-pins.

3. Insert lily and bud in a vertical line of 14" in the back left side. (photo 1) This establishes the height.

4. Insert lilies and buds on the right and left sides of the arrangement close to the edge of the vase, extending about 6" beyond the edge of the pot. (photo 2) These establish the width. Add the fourth lily behind the left one, closer to the center.

5. If the lotus pods have stems, remove them. Insert a wood pick in the side of each one. (photo 3) Insert lotus pods slightly to right of center, one above the other. (photo 4) This establishes visual weight in the center of the arrangement.

Photo 1 - Inserting a lily to establish height.

Photo 2 - Adding lilies for width.

Photo 3 - Inserting a pick in the side of a lotus pod.

6. Insert or glue cones vertically behind the lotus pods. *The cones emphasize the vertical line of the arrangement.*

7. Using the photo as a guide, fill in around the pods with grapes. *The grapes add contrast of color and shape.*

8. Insert berry stems to accent the height and width of the arrangement. *The berries reinforce the vertical and horizontal lines and add movement.*

9. Fill in with sprigs of white statice. ❏

Photo 4 - Placing lotus pods one above the other.

Seasonal Delights

Whether it is the bright yellow of forsythia after a long winter or the
warmth of autumn leaves, each season has special beauty. In this section,
you'll find arrangements that showcase the seasons.

Springtime Garden

A low Oriental-style china container bursts forth with a lush collection of springtime favorites – tulips, forsythia, violets, and plum blossoms. This is my interpretation the vegetative style floral design. In vegetative designs, floral materials are arranged (often in groups) so they resemble growing plants. Only flowers that bloom in the same season would be used together in a vegetative design.

Pictured on page 61

Level of difficulty:

Time to complete:

SUPPLIES

Container:
Low china pot, 7" square, 4" tall

Flowers & Foliage:
2 pink tulips
2 lavender hyacinths
2 stems pink plum blossoms
1 purple African violet
Forsythia
Pink and white wax flower
Green filler flower
Seeded eucalyptus

Other Supplies & Tools:
Green Spanish moss
Knife
Wire cutters
Glue gun and glue
Wood picks
Floral U-pins
Plastic foam or floral foam base material

INSTRUCTIONS

When you place the florals, start in the back of the arrangement and work towards the front. Leave some space between each flower grouping as if they were growing. Allow the flowers and foliage to cascade over the edges of the container. Shape stems in to natural curves for the most realistic look.

1. Trim the base material with a knife to fit the container. The top should be even with the opening of the container.

2. Glue the base material inside container so it fills the opening completely.

3. Cover the base with green Spanish moss. Secure with floral U-pins.

4. Cut tulips to 13" and 11". Insert vertically in the back left corner. (photo 1)

5. Insert plum blossoms to right of tulips to a height of 18". (photo 2)

6. Insert the hyacinth in the center of the arrangement. (photo 3)

7. Insert the forsythia in the right rear corner.

8. Insert the African violet in the left front corner so it hangs over the front to the container slightly.

9. Fill in with the white and pink wax flower, green filler flowers, and seeded eucalyptus. ❑

Spring Flower Facts

- *Spring flowers are some of the most fragrant and colorful of all seasonal flowers. Hyacinths are one of the most fragrant.*

- *As cut flowers, spring flowers are generally not long-lasting.*

- *Tulips are the most widely grown bulb flower with over 3,500 varieties and species. The Netherlands is the world's largest tulip grower. Fresh cut tulips placed in warm will continue to grow toward the light.*

Photo 1 - Inserting the tulips.

Photo 2 - Inserting the plum blossoms.

Photo 3 - Adding the hyacinths.

Carrot Garden

A bright spring arrangement of narcissus and forsythia is tucked inside an unusual container that's easy to make. For the carrot basket, you'll need a recycled plastic tub, artificial carrots, rubber bands, and raffia. (A cottage cheese container is great for this project.)

Level of difficulty:

Time to complete:

SUPPLIES

Container Supplies:

Plastic container, 4" diameter 5" tall

12 plastic carrots

Rubber bands

Sheet moss

Honeysuckle vine

Natural raffia

Flowers, Foliage & Accents:

2 stems forsythia

8 stems narcissus, mini-size

Bear grass

Assorted foliage

Yellow filler flowers

Excelsior

2 Bird eggs

Other Supplies & Tools:

Knife

Wire cutters

Scissors

Glue gun and glue

Floral foam base material (your choice)

INSTRUCTIONS

1. Remove foliage, if any, from carrots. Place a couple of rubber bands around the outside center of the plastic container. Alternating carrots up and down, insert them under the rubber bands, working your way around the container until it is covered.
2. Insert foam base in plastic container. Secure with glue.
3. Glue moss between the carrots to hide the container. Cover foam with moss and glue in place.
4. Shape honeysuckle vine into a handle. Insert in foam and glue in place.
5. Shape excelsior into a bird's nest about 3" in diameter. Glue inside carrot container near front right. Glue eggs in nest.
6. Insert several stems of narcissus in back left side to a height of 9". Add shorter narcissus to fill the left side of the container.
7. Insert stem of forsythia on right side of container to a height of 11".
8. Add foliage and yellow filler flowers, using the photo as a guide.
9. Tie several strands of raffia over the rubber bands. Tie a raffia bow and glue to front center of the container.

Designer's Tips
• *Asparagus, cinnamon sticks, twigs – even pencils – can be used instead of carrots for a fun container.*

• *Printing on plastic food containers can often be removed with mineral spirits or acetone.*

Summer Pitcher

When filled with flowers, ordinary containers have a wonderful, casual charm that fits in almost any room. This casual gathering of summer blossoms is a perfect arrangement for an old pitcher. The ivory dahlias and yellow cosmos look crisp and fresh against the background of bright green viburnum. Starting a casual design with a mass material like viburnum and adding flowers through and above it create depth. Zinnias could be substituted for the dahlias.

I encourage you to give your flowers attitudes – leave some tall and straight; bend others to give them a limp look and allow them to cascade downward. The loose triangle shape of this arrangement works well in almost any tall container.

Level of difficulty: Time to complete:

SUPPLIES

Container:

Metal or pottery pitcher, 8" tall

Flowers:

5 ivory dahlias with buds

6 yellow cosmos with buds

3 green viburnum

3 pale yellow sweet peas

5 green foxtail grass

Assorted foliage (your choice)

Other Supplies & Tools:

Green sheet moss

Knife

Wire cutters

Wood picks

Floral U-pins

Glue gun and glue

Plastic foam or floral foam base material

Optional: Aluminum foil

INSTRUCTIONS

1. *Option:* If you don't want to glue the base material to the pitcher, line it first with aluminum foil.
2. Cut base material to fill inside the pitcher, gluing and wedging in place.
3. Cover base material with green sheet moss. Secure with floral U-pins.
4. Cut the stems of viburnum to about 4" and insert in the center of the pitcher. Shape them so they cascade over the sides of the pitcher.
5. Cut two dahlias to a height of 8". Insert in the center of the pitcher with one bent toward the front and the other to the back. Cut other dahlias to 5" and insert in a circle beneath the taller ones.
6. Using the photo as a guide, insert the cosmos around the dahlias. Bend the stems into curves.
7. Fill in with sweet peas, assorted foliage, and foxtail grass. Have some materials cascading downward over the edge of the pitcher. ❏

Dahlia Facts

Dahlias are a beautiful addition to the landscape. They have a wide height range (1 ft. to 6 ft.) and a variety of flower shapes (single, double, ball). Dahlia blooms range in size from 2" to 12" in shades of orange, pink, purple, red, scarlet, yellow, and white. Some flowers are striped or shaded with a second color. Dahlias bloom from early summer and continue to frost.

Waterfall Arrangement

Waterfall arrangements have long flowing lines with layers of flowers (here I've used pink, purple, and blue ones) and foliage that cascade downward. (Bear grass, asparagus fern, and ivy are often used.) Materials like fibers, thin wires, and feathers are often part of waterfall arrangements. Choose a container that allows the material to flow over the edges easily.

Level of difficulty:

Time to complete:

SUPPLIES

Container:

Tall metal vase in a stand, 13" tall, 5" opening

Flowers & Foliage:

2 pink magnolias

10 orchid lisianthus

7 purple alstromeria

9 blue bachelor buttons

3 lavender larkspur

Purple plum blossoms

Assorted foliage and filler flowers

Other Supplies & Tools:

Wire cutters

Knife

Glue gun and glue

Stones or marbles

Floral U-pins

Floral foam base material

Green sheet moss

INSTRUCTIONS

Shape the flowers into gentle cures before you insert them.

1. Place a handful of stones or marbles in the bottom of the vase for stability.

2. Using the knife, trim the floral base material to fit inside the vase and extend about 1/2" above the opening. Glue in place.

3. Cover base material with moss. Secure with floral U-pins.

4. Insert two larkspur flowing downward about 15" on the left side of the vase.

5. Cut one larkspur in half and insert the pieces on the right side of the vase.

6. Insert two magnolias in the center of the vase with one slightly above the other.

7. Insert plum blossoms close to the larkspur.

8. Using the photo as a guide, insert the lisianthus and alstromeria flowing down the left side of the arrangement.

9. Add foliage, then bachelor buttons and filler flowers.

10. Complete the back of the arrangement with remaining flowers and foliage. ❏

SUPPLIES

Container:

Compote, 8" tall, 7" opening

Flowers, Foliage & Accents:

5 red apples

5 gold pears

3 small gold pears

Assorted berry stems (your choice)

Green viburnum

Asparagus fern

2 shelf mushrooms

Onion grass

Other Supplies & Tools:

Green reindeer moss

Glue gun and glue

Wire cutters

Knife

Awl

Wood picks

Floral foam base material (your choice)

Fruit Compote

This classic arrangement of fruit and flowers is hard to beat.
This combination of red apples and golden pears contrasted with
berries and greens would be beautiful on the dining table
or a kitchen counter.
In this arrangement I did not need to cover the base material
with moss because the materials cover the entire surface.

Level of difficulty:

Time to complete:

INSTRUCTIONS

You'll need to insert wood picks in each piece of fruit before placing it. Vary the location of the pick to work with how the fruit will be placed in the arrangement (some fruits will be vertical, others on their sides).

1. Trim floral base material to fit container and extend about 1/2" above the opening. Glue in place.

2. Insert shelf mushrooms, placing (terracing) them one above the other in the center front of the container.

3. Insert and glue a cluster of three pears in center of container.

4. Attach a wood pick to the stem of one pear and insert and glue it so it hangs over the container edge on the left side.

5. Using the photo as a guide insert the apples around the pears.

6. Insert the small pears around the apples.

7. Fill in around the fruits with berries, sprigs of asparagus fern, and pieces of viburnum.

8. Insert onion grass cascading downward on the right and front left of the arrangement.

9. Hide any glue and fill empty spaces with reindeer moss. ❑

Garden Romance

This garden design is a great example of how to create a large scale arrangement. It includes a wide variety of flowers in related colors, and it is easier than you think! You have the option of arranging the flowers directly in the vase or on a tray that sits on top of the vase. I like to use a tray – that way the arrangement can be displayed in different ways and I can use the vase for another arrangement, if needed.

Level of difficulty:

Time to complete:

SUPPLIES

Container:
Vase, 10" tall, 6" wide
Optional: Tray or saucer that will sit on the vase opening

Flowers & Foliage:
7 Stock - 4 purple, 3 white (line)
4 Ivory magnolias (form)
5 Open yellow roses (form)
5 Pink peonies (mass)
5 Ivory rose buds (form)
Assorted line, mass, form, and filler flowers (your choice)
Assorted foliage (your choice)

Other Supplies & Tools:
Wire cutters
Knife
Glue gun and glue
Sheet moss
Floral U-pins
Wood picks
Floral foam (your choice)

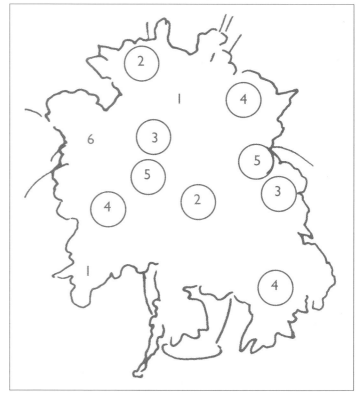

1. Stock 2. Ivory magnolia 3. Open yellow rose
4. Pink peony 5. Ivory rosebud

Instructions begin on page 72

INSTRUCTIONS

In large arrangements I like to put glue on each stem as I insert it to make the finished arrangement more secure. This is a radiating design – all the stems should appear to be coming from one point at the center of the vase.

1. Fill either the vase or the tray with foam base material and glue it in place.

2. Cover foam with moss. Secure with floral U-pins.

3. Insert a cluster of three stock in middle of the foam base at a height at least one-and-one-half times the vase height. (photo 1) Insert the remaining stock equally spaced around the bottom edge. (The stock establish the shape and overall size of the arrangement.)

4. Insert the magnolias, placing one centered in the front very close to the foam. (This helps create depth – you insert the largest flower first, followed by the next in size, and so on.) Insert the other magnolias equally spaced throughout the arrangement.

5. Insert the peonies – one to the lower right front and the others equally spaced in the arrangement.

6. Hang the plums as a guide – two in the upper part of the arrangement. (Step back and study the arrangement. Do the colors look balanced? They should appear random, not lined up. Adjust as needed for a more random look.)

7. Add foliage to fill in around the flowers. Adjust the stems to have a little curve.

8. Insert the remaining flowers around the larger blossoms, allowing some to cascade downward for a full, lush look.

9. Insert some grass to extend beyond the flowers to add texture and movement. ❏

Designer's Tips for Large Arrangements

• *Use a variety of flower shapes.*

• *Start with the line flowers to establish the shape. Follow with the largest flowers, placing some large flowers close to the foam base to create depth. (Hydrangeas are great for creating depth.)*

• *Place the large flowers so each has its own space, with no two large flowers touching one another.*

• *Place lighter colors near the edges of the arrangement.*

• *Cutting the stems apart and adding the blossoms and buds to wood picks gives you more options for placement.*

• *Don't be afraid to prune away extra foliage on flower stems.*

Photo 1 - The stock establishes the height of the arrangement.

If you create the Garden Romance arrangement on a tray, it can be displayed on different vases or even a large candlestick, as shown here.

Ledge Garden

Ledge gardens are a wonderful way to add color, texture, and softness to otherwise hard-to-decorate spaces – ledge gardens are great on top of cabinets, on a high book shelf, or on the sill of a window without a view.

Level of difficulty:

Time to complete:

SUPPLIES

Container:
Planter box, 30" long, 5" tall, 6" wide

Foliage:
Boston fern
Wandering Jew
Heart ivy
Other plants (your choice)

Other Supplies & Tools:
Moss
Floral U-pins
Knife
Glue gun and glue
Wire cutters
Wood picks
Floral foam base material (your choice)

Designer's Tips For Ledge Gardens

• *Cutting the plant materials into small sections will allow you to arrange them more easily.*

• *Choose plants with contrasting leaf shapes, sizes, and colors.*

• *Choose plants that are both upright and cascading in their growth patterns.*

• *For the most realistic look, choose plants that naturally grow in the same space.*

• *If the arrangement will be displayed above eye level, use vining plants and keep them toward the front edge of the container, as the back will not be seen. As you work, periodically place the container where you intend to display it to check the perspective.*

• *A ledge garden can be made on a sheet of plastic foam (Styrofoam®) if the container will not be seen. For added weight and to keep it from tipping forward, glue the foam to a piece of wooden shelving or a heavy scrap of plywood.*

INSTRUCTIONS

Oftentimes less IS more. Don't crowd your plants; allow each its own space.

1. Fill container with floral base material and glue in place.

2. Cover base material with moss. Secure with floral U-pins.

3. Cut apart the fern and insert sections at the left end of the container. Shape the leaves into smooth arcs.

4. Insert heart ivy at right end of container and shape stems.

5. Establish the height with a plant of your choice next to the ivy.

6. Insert wandering Jew to left of fern. Shape stems carefully. ❏

Framed Florals

Tight clusters of dried materials, berries, and blossoms create a rich textural
surface in this unusual arrangement.
For a design variation, fill a frame or a low, shallow container with shapes of
mini carnations, small mums, and sweetheart roses.

Level of difficulty: Time to complete:

SUPPLIES

Container:

Wicker or wooden picture frame (your choice), 9" x 12"

Flowers, Foliage & Accents:

3 small protea flats

6 small lotus pods

15 hazelnuts

10 olive green artificial grapes

12 stems bearded natural wheat

Tallow berry stems (artificial)

Red preserved eucalyptus

4 small natural-cut palmettos

Assorted orange berry stems

Red orange small blossoms (e.g., from delphinium or hydrangea)

Yellow filler flower

Artificial grapevine

Other Supplies & Tools:

Glue gun and glue

Wire cutters

Knife

Plastic foam (Styrofoam®), 1" thick, cut to the size of the frame opening

Wood picks

Optional: Glossy wood-tone spray

INSTRUCTIONS

1. Using a knife, trim the foam to fit snugly inside the opening of the picture frame. Glue in place.

2. Cut stems of palmetto short so, when inserted in the foam base, they lay on the surface. Insert palmetto stems in a diagonal line. (photo 1)

3. Cut stems of protea flats short. Insert and glue in place, letting them extend off the left corner of the frame. (photo 2)

4. Cut stems of lotus pods and insert. (If your lotus pods do not have stems, glue each on a wood pick.)

5. Fill in to the right of the palmetto with tips of red eucalyptus and red orange blossoms.

6. Follow with a row of grapes.

7. Glue in hazelnuts and orange berries around the lotus pods. Trim the beards of the wheat short and insert and glue to the left of the lotus pods.

8. Shape stems of tallow berries and insert and glue to outline the palmetto.

9. Fill in around the tallow berries with yellow filler flowers.

10. Insert two lengths of grapevine to twist across the arrangement.

11. *Optional:* Spray with glossy wood-tone spray to enhance the color and seal.

Photo 1 - Inserting the palmetto.

Photo 2 - Inserting protea.

Pumpkin Patch

A ceramic pumpkin with the lid perched among the flowers makes this simple design of sunflowers a seasonal beauty. Designing in an unusual container is a great way to display a few flowers. I'll show you how to add a removable liner and secure a lid to an arrangement in this project.

Level of difficulty:

Time to complete:

SUPPLIES

Container:
Ceramic pumpkin with lid, 5" tall, 6" opening
Plastic liner (to fit inside pumpkin)

Flowers & Foliage:
4 large sunflowers with buds
Bittersweet
Dried (or dried-looking) hydrangea
Brown magnolia leaves
Bear grass

Other Supplies & Tools:
Green floral tape
Wire cutters
Glue gun and glue
Wood picks
Sheet moss
Floral U-pins
Knife
Hole punch
Chenille stems
Waterproof adhesive tape
Heavy stem wires
Floral foam base material

Instructions begin on page 80.

INSTRUCTIONS

1. Using a hole punch, make holes on opposite sides of the liner near the top. (photo 1)

2. Twist a chenille stem through each hole and form a loop to act as a handle. (photo 2) This allows you to grasp and remove the liner from the container easily.

3. Trim the floral base material to fit the liner. Glue in place.

4. Cover with sheet moss. Secure with floral U-pins. Place the liner in the pumpkin. (photo 3)

5. Form a heavy stem wire to fit the inside of the lid, letting the ends of the wire extend from the lid, and attach it to a wooden pick with floral tape. (photo 4)

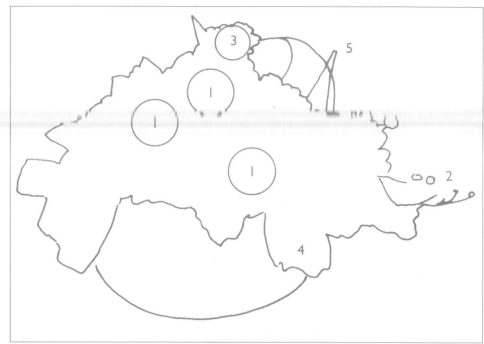

1. Sunflower 2. Bittersweet 3. Hydrangea 4. Brown magnolia leaf 5. Bear grass

Photo 1 - Punching holes in the liner.

Photo 2 - The liner with chenille-stem loop handles attached.

6. With waterproof tape, secure the wire inside the lid under the rim. (photo 5)

7. Insert the pick attached to the lid on the left side of the pumpkin.

8. Insert a circle of magnolia leaves around the edge of the liner.

9. Cut the stems of the sunflowers and buds to about 3". Insert in a tight circle in the center. Secure the stems with glue if they are large.

10. Fill in around the sunflowers close to the base material with hydrangea.

11. Using the photo as a guide, insert stems of bittersweet.

12. Attach a wood pick to each end of a cluster of bear grass and insert into the arrangement so the grass arcs across the sunflowers. ❏

Photo 3 - The liner inside the container, with foam base material in place.

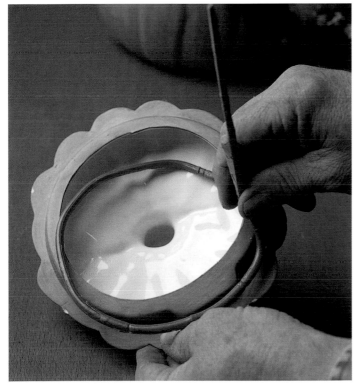

Photo 4 - Preparing the shaped wire, with wood pick attached, to fit inside the lid.

Photo 5 - Securing the wire under the rim of the lid with strips of waterproof tape.

Christmas Gathering

Wouldn't this rustic basket filled with evergreens, berries, pine cones, and apples be the perfect addition to a fireplace mantel? Using silk greens and artificial apples ensures this arrangement will be beautiful for many years.

Level of difficulty:

Time to complete:

SUPPLIES

Container:

Wicker basket with handle, 14" long, 8" deep, 11" tall with handle

Flowers, Foliage & Accents:

7 large red apples

12 green crabapples

8 pine cones

Red and green berry sprays

Evergreens (your choice)

Assorted foliage (I used magnolia leaves and seeded eucalyptus.)

Red eucalyptus

Other Supplies & Tools:

4 yds. red plaid wire-edge ribbon, 2-1/2" wide

Knife

Wire cutters

Scissors

Awl

Floral wire

Wood picks

Glue gun and glue

Floral foam base material (your choice)

Optional: Black plastic bag

INSTRUCTIONS

1. *Option:* Line basket with a black plastic bag to keep bits of foam from coming through the basket.

2. Place foam in basket. Trim foam so it fills the basket and is level with the opening. Use wire or tape across the top of foam to hold the foam in place.

3. Insert evergreens extending about 8" on either end of the basket and shape so they flow downward.

4. Fill the rest of the basket with short sprigs of greens, keeping them below the handle.

5. Using an awl, make holes in apples and insert and glue picks. Insert the apples at the center of the basket.

6. Cut a 1-1/2 yd. length of ribbon and form a four-loop bow with 4" loops and 6" streamers. Secure bow with floral wire and attach to a wood pick. Insert bow to left of the handle close to the edge.

7. Form the remaining ribbon into three sets of loops secured on a wood pick. Insert loops in the foam base, one on the front right, one on the back left, and one on the back right. Trim ends of ribbons in V-shapes.

8. Using the photo as guide, glue pine cones, berries, and green apples in place.

9. Glue in sprigs of red eucalyptus. ❑

Designer's Tips

• *If the apples and berries seem a bit bright, spray them lightly with a glossy wood-tone spray.*

• *Do you have a Christmas arrangement that is faded and maybe a little tired? To refresh, spray lightly with a clear acrylic spray and sprinkle with clear diamond dust for a frosted look.*

Golden Glow

Broken shade on your candelabrum? No problem – simply replace it with a floral design in glowing gilded fruits, golden berries, and sheer metallic ribbon. Gold is a traditional Christmas favorite and in candlelight the glow of gold is always lovely. A silver candelabrum would be equally pretty with silver fruits and icy accents.

Level of difficulty: Time to complete:

SUPPLIES

Container:

Brass candelabrum for two candles
   (You'll use one shade and candle.)

Foliage & Accents:

2 gold beaded or gilded apples

2 gold beaded or gilded pears

Assorted golden berry sprays

Assorted pine and spruce greenery

Other Supplies & Tools:

2 yds. sheer gold metallic ribbon,
   2-1/2" wide

Plastic foam (Styrofoam®) ball, 2-1/2"

Glue gun and glue

Wire cutters

Scissors

Knife

Wood picks

Awl

INSTRUCTIONS

1. Remove glass shade and candle. Set aside while making the arrangement.

2. Press foam ball on the left candle holder. Remove ball. Using a knife, carve a hole in ball so it will fit over the candle holder. Glue hollowed ball in place.

3. Insert short lengths of spruce and pine in the ball to a height of 6" on the back left side and cascading to the front right.

4. Using an awl, insert picks in apples and pears. Insert the apples and pears in a tight cluster centered in the greens as shown.

5. Cut a 1-yd. length of ribbon. Form a two-loop bow with 4" loops and 6" streamers. Attach bow to wood pick and insert into arrangement at lower left. Make a second bow and place on the back right. Trim ends of ribbon in V-shapes.

6. Fill in around the ribbon with berries, shaping the berries so they flow downward.

7. Glue in additional sprigs of greenery, if needed, so the arrangement looks full and lush.

8. Replace candle and shade. ❏

Designer's Tips

• *If you don't want to place the arrangement permanently on the candle holder, wrap the candle holder with aluminum foil before gluing the foam ball – you'll be able to remove the arrangement easily.*

• *Using pre-made sprays of fruits and berries makes this type of design easy. Use the entire spray or cut into smaller sections.*

• *Recycle faded fruits and berries by spraying with metallic paint. While the paint is wet, sprinkle with tiny clear beads or glitter for sparkle.*

Topiaries

Topiaries always seem special – the sculptured shapes of flowers and foliage atop stems are an out-of-the-ordinary presentation. On the following pages, you'll see two topiary arrangements that are easy to make and a delight to display.

Mille fleur Topiary

The variety of flowers, colors, and textures in this topiary makes it a beautiful focal point for almost any room. It's a great project to make when you have flower heads that have fallen from their stems, flowers with short stems, and odds and ends of blossoms. You could also purchase bushes and mixed sprays of flowers to yield a large quantity of blossoms economically.

Choose a variety of mass, form, and filler flowers for a lush, colorful display.

Pictured on page 89

Level of difficulty:

Time to complete: 🕐 🕐 🕐

SUPPLIES

Container:

Terra cotta bulb pot, 8" diameter, 4-1/2" tall

Flowers & Foliage:

Curly willow stems, 20" long

Silk flowers - I used roses, coneflowers, daisies, hydrangea, magnolia, and statice, among others.

Assorted foliage

Other Supplies & Tools:

Sheet moss

Reindeer moss

Knife

Glue gun and glue

Wire cutters

Pruning shears

Floral U-pins

Plastic foam (Because of the many heavy stems, this works best.)

Duct tape

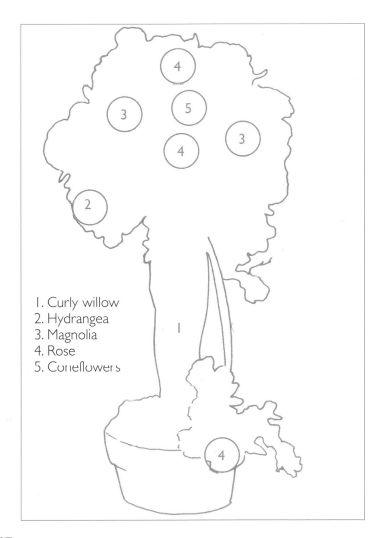

1. Curly willow
2. Hydrangea
3. Magnolia
4. Rose
5. Coneflowers

INSTRUCTIONS

1. Cover the hole in the bottom of the pot with duct tape.

2. Using a knife, trim the foam level with the top of the pot. Glue in place.

3. Cover foam with sheet moss. Place reindeer moss around the edges.

4. Insert several stems of curly willow in the center of the pot to a height of about 18". (photo 1) Trim stems as needed with pruning shears.

5. Cut two pieces of foam about 6" long. Glue together to form a piece 4" deep. Bevel edges of foam.

6. Insert foam on curly willow stems. (photo 2) Squirt hot glue around stems.

7. Cover the foam piece on the stems with sheet moss. Secure with floral U-pins.

8. Starting with the largest ones, insert flowers in the foam on the top of the stems. Follow with next largest flowers, then the smaller flowers. Finish with filler flowers. Place the colors evenly for variety.

9. Add foliage for contrast and to fill the empty spaces.

10. Insert a small cluster of flowers at the base of the stems. ❏

Photo 1 - Inserting the last curly willow stem.

Photo 2 - Placing the foam block on top of the willow stems.

Sunflower Topiary

This topiary is so simple – a few stems of sunflowers are bound together for a bold, bright arrangement. Almost any type flower can be clustered and used as topiary; roses, alstromeria, and carnations (both fresh and silk) all work well.

Level of difficulty:

Time to complete:

SUPPLIES

Container:

Moss covered pot, 7" diameter, 6" tall

Flowers:

3 sunflower stems, each with
   2 flowers and a bud

Other Supplies & Tools:

Natural raffia

Sheet moss

Wire cutters

Floral U-pins

Knife

Scissors

Glue gun and glue

Plastic foam

INSTRUCTIONS

1. Trim plastic foam with a knife so it fits inside the pot and is level with top.

2. Cover the foam with sheet moss. Secure with floral U-pins.

3. Cut two sunflowers and two buds from different stems and set aside.

4. Hold all the sunflower stems in a cluster and adjust the heads and buds so they form a rounded shape. Insert the stems as one, centered in the pot, to a height of 24". Squirt hot glue around the stems to secure.

5. Take several strands of raffia and, starting just below the blossoms, wrap the raffia around the stems, working your way down to the pot. Secure with a knot and glue near the moss.

6. Insert the reserved flowers and buds, with one flower slightly taller than the other, near the front edge of the pot. ❏

Arrangements
in Clear Containers

Flowers arranged in glass vases showcase the sculptural quality of the stems. Whether you support the flowers with a filler like beans or marbles, choose faux water, or swirl the flowers inside the vase, flowers and clear glass are a clearly beautiful combination. Some say using glass vases is difficult, but on the following pages I will show you easy ways to create this fresh look.

Garden Vase

Garden arrangements are mixed flower bouquets that have a just-picked freshness. This timeless combination of pale and bright pastels is arranged in a clear glass vase filled with sparkling water. The trumpet shape of the vase makes arranging a mixture of line, form, and filler flowers easy. The water is an acrylic resin you pour and let set. Choose a work surface where the project can remain undisturbed for 48 hours. You could also follow the instructions for the European Hand Tied Bouquet to arrange the flowers, then drop the bouquet in the resin.

Level of difficulty:

Time to complete:

The acrylic resin takes about 48 hours to dry.

SUPPLIES

Clear glass trumpet vase 11" high with a 5" opening

Flowers:

Choose only flowers with plastic coated stems; paper-wrapped stems will not work.

5 pale pink rosebuds   5 snapdragons - 3 pink, 2 orchid

5 pink sweet pea stems   4 purple anemones

4 purple coneflowers   Pink and purple filler flowers

Other Supplies & Tools:

Green glass gems

Clear acrylic resin water, about 15 oz.

Wire cutters

Waterproof bowl tape

Disposable mixing bowl (a food storage container works well)

Wooden spoon

Latex gloves

Newspapers or drop cloth

Paper towels   Soap and water

Matte acrylic sealer   Small artist's brush

Small plastic funnel   Knife

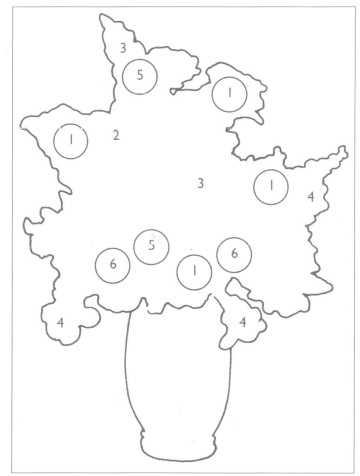

1. Pale pink rosebud 2. Pink snapdragon
3. Orchid snapdragon 4. Pink sweet pea
5. Purple anemone 6. Purple coneflower

INSTRUCTIONS

1. Clean the vase and glass gems with soap and water. Dry thoroughly.

2. Place gems in the vase to a depth of about 2". (The gems take up space so you can use less acrylic resin, and they add weight so the arrangement is not top heavy.)

3. Insert the snapdragons, centered in the vase, to a height of about 16" above the vase opening.

4. Cutting the stems as needed, insert the roses, anemones, and coneflowers around the snapdragons so the stems spiral outward.

5. Fill in with sweet peas and filler flowers, adjusting the stems and blossoms as needed. Be sure each stem reaches the glass gems in the bottom of the vase. Remove any foliage that will be beneath the "water."

6. Carefully remove the flowers as a bunch. Tape together as one near where the top of the vase was on the stems.

7. Using an artist's brush, coat the bottom half of the stems with acrylic sealer. Allow to dry. (This keeps the stems from bleeding color into the acrylic resin.)

8. Spread newspapers or a drop cloth on your work surface. Wearing latex gloves, mix the acrylic resin according to the package instructions. Stir the mixture thoroughly. (photo 1)

9. Using the funnel, slowly pour the acrylic resin into the vase, being careful not to splash any resin on the sides of the vase. (photo 2)

10. Place the bouquet back in the vase, being sure all the stems are in the acrylic resin. Allow the project to dry undisturbed for 48 hours. (It could take longer, depending on the temperature and humidity.)

11. When the resin is set, cut the tape from the flowers and shape the bouquet as needed. ❏

Photo 1 - Mixing the resin.

Designer's Tips: Mixed Flower Bouquets

• *An arrangement made up of only soft pastels can have a faded look. For contrast, add a touch of bright green or purple.*

• *Scatter colors so you don't have straight lines of any one color.*

• *Softer colors like blue and pale lavender will recede while bolder pinks and yellow will advance.*

• *Remember to add weight to taller vases so they are balanced, not top heavy.*

Photo 2 - Pouring the resin through a funnel into the vase.

Pavé Rose Bouquet

Pavé is a French term borrowed from jewelry making where stones are set so closely together that no metal shows. In pave floral designs, flowers and other materials are set so closely together that no base material is seen and the materials all touch one another. Pave designs have rich texture and a lush look. The arrangements are low, no higher than the top of the container. This type of arrangement highlights the blooms instead of the shape of the arrangement or the leaves and stems.

When creating a pave design, start with the largest flowers. Follow with the next largest, working your way to the smallest ones. Keep the florals close and compact with flowers touching one another.

SUPPLIES

Container:

Clear glass rectangular vase, 3" wide, 4" high

Flowers:

15 - 18 rosebuds or tight small roses (NOTE: Choose flowers with plastic coated stems only. Flowers with paper-wrapped stems will not work with the resin.)

Other Supplies & Tools:

Green glass gems or half-marbles

Clear acrylic resin water (about 5 oz.)

Wire cutters

Disposable mixing bowl (a food storage container works well)

Wooden spoon

Latex gloves

Newspapers or drop cloth

Paper towels

Soap and water

Acrylic matte sealer

Small artist's brush

Small plastic funnel

Level of difficulty:

Time to complete:

(The acrylic resin takes about 48 hours to dry.)

INSTRUCTIONS

Choose a work surface where the project can remain undisturbed for 48 hours.

1. Clean the vase and glass gems with soap and water. Dry thoroughly.

2. Place gems in the vase to a depth of about 1". (The gems take up space so you use less acrylic resin.)

3. Using wire cutters, trim the stems of the roses to about 5" so they rest just above the opening of the vase.

4. Using the artist's brush, apply acrylic sealer to the bottom half of the stems. Allow to dry. (Sealing keeps the stems from bleeding color into the acrylic resin.)

5. Spread newspapers or a drop cloth on work surface. Wearing latex gloves, mix the acrylic resin according to the package instructions. Stir the mixture thoroughly.

6. Using the funnel, slowly pour the acrylic resin into the vase, being careful not to splash resin on the sides of the vase.

7. Insert the roses in the vase. Be sure all the stems are in the acrylic resin. Allow the project to dry undisturbed for 48 hours. (It could take longer, depending on temperature and humidity.)

8. When the resin is dry, shape the roses. ❑

Poppy Duo

I love poppies – their translucent color and tissue thin texture always look happy. In this contemporary pairing, two arrangements complement each other and the beauty of the poppy with the sparkle of glass.

Level of difficulty:

Time to complete:

SUPPLIES

Containers:

Oblong glass vase, 7" tall, 9" wide at opening, 4" deep

Square glass vase, 3" tall, 3" deep, 4" wide

Flowers:

5 orange poppies and buds

Bear grass

Other Supplies & Tools:

Wire cutters

Glue gun and glue

Dried beans (I used lima beans, kidney beans, and black beans.)

INSTRUCTIONS

For the small vase:

1. Fill small vase level with the opening with the bean of your choice.

2. Cut one poppy to a stem length of 2" and insert in back right corner.

3. Cut another poppy stem to a length of 5" and insert in front right corner. Shape stem downward.

4. Insert two buds extending from the right side.

5. Curl a piece of cut stem and insert on the left side.

6. Squirt a little hot glue around the stems of all the flowers where they are inserted in the beans.

For large vase:

1. Fill large glass vase with layers of beans level with the opening.

2. Cut one poppy bud stem to 12" and another 9". Insert buds vertically in back left corner.

3. Cut two poppy blossoms to 5". Insert one in back of vase and other curved in front.

4. Insert last blossom in the left corner.

5. Add other bud curving to the left side.

6. Add bear grass around the vertical poppies. Glue as needed. ❑

Daisy Delight

Canning jars, old medicine bottles – even glass baby bottles – are great containers for arrangements. Let the stems show through the bottle or, as I did here, fill the bottle with green split peas. The peas hold the stems in place and do no damage to the bottle. Using a variety of foliage (different sizes, colors, and shapes) gives your arrangement texture, visual interest, and a polished, professional look. Here, grasses and herbs contrast with the ivy. I think this arrangement would be pretty on a kitchen counter or as a hostess gift.

Level of difficulty: Time to complete:

SUPPLIES

Container:

Glass jar

Flowers & Foliage:

5 black-eyed susans

6 orange and yellow small daisy type flowers

5 orange ranunculus

Red orange berry sprays

Assorted grasses, herbs, and ivy

Other Supplies & Tools:

Wire cutters

Green split peas

Optional: Clear packaging tape

INSTRUCTIONS

1. Fill the jar within 1/2" of the opening with green split peas and pack the peas tightly in the jar.

2. *Option:* To keep the peas from spilling, cover the opening with clear tape and insert the stems through the tape into the peas.

3. Insert one black-eyed susan centered to a height of about 10" from the opening of the jar.

4. Insert a circle of three black-eyed susans to a height of 7" around the tallest one.

5. Add the remaining black-eyed susan slightly above the container opening. Shape all the flower stems so they point outward.

6. Fill in around the black-eyed susans with ranunculus.

7. Follow with assorted foliage.

8. Add the orange daisies.

9. Insert clusters of berries. ❏

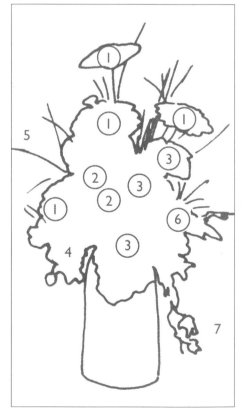

1. Black-eyed susan 2. Orange and yellow daisy 3. Orange ranunculus
4. Red orange berries 5. Grass
6. Herb 7. Ivy

European Hand-Tied Bouquet

European hand tied bouquets are loose gatherings of flowers that are bound together. The stems rotate in a spiral that adds fullness and gives a just-picked look, and the spiraling stems will support the bouquet even without a container.
This type of bouquet is easy to just drop in a vase, so it makes a great gift when presented wrapped in tissue and tied with a bow.

Level of difficulty: ❀ ❀

Time to complete: ⏰

SUPPLIES

Container:
Glass vase (your choice)

Flowers & Foliage:
4 White larkspur (line)
3 White lilies with buds (form)
5 White viburnum (mass)
3 White poppies (mass)
White filler flowers and berries

Other Supplies & Tools:
Cable tie
Floral tape
Wire cutters

Instructions begin on page 104.

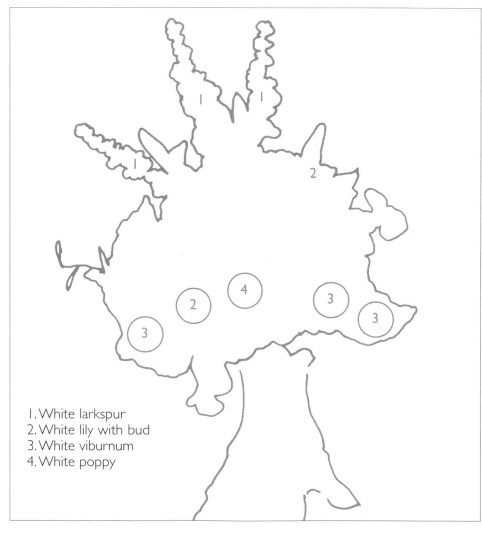

1. White larkspur
2. White lily with bud
3. White viburnum
4. White poppy

INSTRUCTIONS

When making this arrangement, hold the flowers and greenery midway up the stems between your thumb and index finger in your non-dominant hand. Keep your hands relaxed. (Believe it or not, you have more control that way.)

1. Remove the leaves from the lower half of all the stems.

2. Start the bouquet with the larkspur; by doing this, the larkspur will end up in the center of the bouquet.

3. Pick up a viburnum. Place it directly on the larkspur at a 45-degree angle. (Photo 1) Turn the bouquet in your hand one-quarter of a turn. By placing the stems at a 45-degree angle, you create a spiral of stems that will stand up like a teepee.

4. Continue adding viburnum, lily, and poppy stems, each at an angle, turning the bouquet in a clockwise direction. (Photo 2) Finish with the filler flowers.

5. When you have added all the flowers fasten the bouquet with a cable tie at the point where your hand was holding the flowers. (Photo 3) Trim cable tie end. Cover cable tie with floral tape.

6. Trim the stems evenly so they will rest flat at the bottom of the vase.

7. Place the bouquet in the vase and adjust as needed. ❏

Photo 1 - Adding a viburnum stem at a 45-degree angle.

Photo 2 - Adding a lily.

Photo 3 - Attaching the cable tie.

Classic Calla Lilies

In this contemporary design, the calla lilies reflect the shape of a clear glass pedestal bowl. This arrangement is a "mono-botanical" design – one that uses only one type of flower to showcase the beauty of that flower.
This type arrangement can be made with fresh flowers or faux. When using fresh calla lilies, leave them out of water for a while until their stems become pliable. If you're using artificial ones, be sure the stems are flexible.

Level of difficulty:

Time to complete: 🕰

SUPPLIES

Container:
Clear glass pedestal bowl, 7" tall, 9" diameter

Flowers & Foliage:
4 calla lilies
Artificial willow stems

Other Supplies & Tools:
Clear glass gems
Green floral tape that matches flower stems
Wire cutters

INSTRUCTIONS

1. Shape the stems of the calla lilies into curves. If you have trouble shaping the stems of artificial flowers, warm them in hot water to soften the plastic and make them more pliable.

2. Starting with the lily nearest the center of the vase, twist the stem and insert it so it is wedged inside the bowl.

3. Working from right to left, swirl the other calla lilies inside and slightly above the opening of the bowl. Trim the stems as needed to keep the flowers wedged inside.

4. Tape the cut ends with floral tape.

5. Twist the stems of willow around the flowers.

6. Place glass gems inside the bowl around the flower stems. ❑

Designer's Tip
• *Always* lift bowls by their side and bottom, lifting by the rim may cause the bowl to break especially if it is filled with water or a heavy arrangement.

Calla Lily Facts
The flower known as the calla or arum lily isn't a true lily. A South African native, each long stem has a solitary flower consisting of a thick, yellowish spadix enveloped in a delicate spathe, most often white or cream. Callas grow in a wide variety of colors besides the familiar white and cream, including pinks, purples, and yellows.

Holiday Fun

For the holidays, using non-traditional colors (chartreuse, blue, and hot pink) surrounding a chartreuse candle atop a glass vase is a sure way to attract attention. You could, of course, substitute traditional greens, reds, and golds, but isn't the unexpected a bit more fun?

Level of difficulty:    Time to complete:

SUPPLIES

Container:

Glass cylinder vase, 12" tall,
   4" diameter

Plastic tray that will sit upside down
   on vase (I used a 5" plant saucer.)

Flowers, Foliage & Accents:

3 purple delphiniums

Hot pink glittered fern

Evergreens (your choice)

Green filler flower

Assorted glass ornaments -
   Chartreuse, hot pink, blues

Other Supplies & Tools:

3 yds. purple sheer ribbon,
   1-1/2" wide

Plastic candle holder, 3"

Chartreuse pillar candle, 3" x 9"

Plastic foam

Glue gun and glue

Scissors

Wire cutters

Floral wire

Knife

Wood picks

INSTRUCTIONS

1. Place ornaments inside vase.
2. Place saucer upside down on opening of the vase. (Upside down, it won't slide easily.)
3. Trim plastic floral foam and glue to saucer.
4. Insert and glue candle holder in center of the foam.
5. Insert evergreens in the foam to hide the saucer, foam, and candle holder.
6. Insert two delphiniums at left cascading downward 14".
7. Insert glitter ferns under the delphiniums. Add a cluster on the right side.
8. Using the photo as guide, glue ornaments around the candle holder.
9. Twist a floral wire on two ornaments and suspend them from the evergreens on the left front.
10. Cut the ribbon into two 1-1/2 yd. lengths. Form each length into a two-loop bow with 5" loops and 12" streamers. Secure with floral wire and attach each to a wood pick.
11. Insert one bow at back left. Insert the other at front right.
12. Glue green filler flowers and additional balls as desired.
13. Place candle in holder.

Designer's Tips

• *Candles can be painted with floral spray paints or acrylic paint designed for candles. Both are safe to burn when dry.*

• *Vary this arrangement by using more traditional colors like gold and ivory, or make a summer arrangement with lemons instead of holiday ornaments and ivy instead of evergreens.*

Candles & Flowers

I love to use candles with flowers, whether they are tall tapers, flickering votives, or chunky pillars, to add romance, movement, and drama to arrangements. Using good sense and the proper techniques makes your finished designs beautiful and safe.
You can use plastic candle holders to secure candles in bases (just choose a holder that fits your candle(s) or add picks to the bottom of a candle with floral adhesive clay.

To insert a candle holder in foam base material, apply glue to the spiked end and press the spike in the base material. Be sure the holder is level and secure, and place the candle in the holder. (I like to insert the candles before I start arranging the florals. That way, I can keep the flowers in proportion to the candles as I create the arrangement.

Pictured above, clockwise from top left: Plastic pillar holder, wood picks, a plastic taper holder in foam base material, plastic taper holders, floral adhesive clay on a roll.

Using Wooden Picks to Secure a Candle

1. Place a strip of floral adhesive clay around the bottom of the candle. (photo 1)

2. Press wooden picks, equally spaced, into the clay with the pointed ends of the picks extending beyond the bottom of the candle. (photo 2)

3. Wrap waterproof adhesive tape around the candle over the clay strips and picks.

4. Insert candle in floral base. Be sure candle is level and secure. (Photo 3) ❏

Photo 1 - Placing the floral adhesive clay strip.

Photo 2 - Pressing the wooden picks into the clay.

Photo 3 - Inserting the candle in the floral base.

Candle Tips

• *Never leave a candle burning unattended.*

• *To extinguish a burning candle and prevent wax from spraying, use a candle snuffer or hold your index finger close to the flame and blow around your finger gently.*

• *Keep the wick centered and trimmed to 1/4".*

• *Do not allow matches, trimmed wicks, or other objects to remain in the candle.*

• *Store candles in a cool place. Cool wax burns longer. Candles can be placed in the freezer before burning to increase their burn time.*

• *Allow pillar and votive candles to burn until the wax reaches the outer edge. With pillars this could take one to four hours.*

• *To remove drips of candle wax from a tablecloth, wait for the wax to cool, and then scrape off as much wax as you can with a dull knife. Place a couple of white paper towels over the remaining wax and run a warm iron over the drip(s). Repeat, using clean paper towels each time, until all the wax is gone.*

• *Polish candles by rubbing with a soft cloth or a fine mesh cloth.*

• *To prevent fading, keep candles out of direct sunlight.*

Taper Candle Herb Garden

The gray-green foliage and galvanized containers contrast with the yellow flowers and straight lines of the taper candles. This arrangement would be great on a patio table, a kitchen counter, or a dining room buffet. You can make an even quicker, easier version – Simply buy arrangements of greens in small pots (from a craft, gift, or floral shop) and add some flowers and candles.

Level of difficulty:

Time to complete:

SUPPLIES

Container:

3 galvanized metal pots and tray
(The tray is 14" long and 5" wide. Each pot is 5" tall and 4" wide.)

Flowers & Foliage:

8 yellow cosmos

3 yellow ranunculus

Pale yellow berry spray

12 lavender stems

Assorted gray green herb-like foliage

Other Supplies & Tools:

3 plastic taper candle holder picks

3 ivory taper candles 15"

Base material (your choice – plastic or floral foam)

Spanish moss

Green reindeer moss

Knife

Wire cutters

Glue gun and glue

Floral U-pins

INSTRUCTIONS

1. Glue the pots, spacing them equally, in the tray.

2. Trim some base material to fit inside each pot and glue in place.

3. Cover the top of each pot with Spanish moss. Secure with floral U-pins.

4. Insert and glue a candle holder in center of each pot.

5. Insert herb-like greens vertically to a height of about 6" in each pot. Shape some of the greens so they hang over the edges of the pots.

6. Using the photo as a guide, insert three yellow cosmos in the left side of the left pot at heights of 9", 7", and 3". Insert two cosmos on the right side of the right pot at heights of 6" and 4" and two more that cascade downward. Insert one cosmos in the center pot.

7. Cut ranunculus stems to lengths of 4". Insert two in the left pot and two in the right pot.

8. Insert stems of lavender vertically in the back of both the left and center pots. Insert some lavender in the front left of the right pot.

9. Insert berries, letting them cascade downward.

10. Glue Spanish moss in tray around the base of each pot. Add reindeer moss as desired.

11. Place one taper candle in each holder. ❑

Harvest Centerpiece

This long and low centerpiece of autumn flowers and candles is a classic dining
table design. If centerpiece will be on the table during a meal, be sure
it is low enough that guests can see over it.
Plastic foam (Styrofoam®) works best as the base for this arrangement
because of the candle holders and heavy stems.

SUPPLIES

Container:

Brown ceramic bowl, 4" tall, 8"
    diameter opening

Flowers, Foliage & Accents:

3 large yellow pears

2 small yellow pears

Bunch of green grapes

3 orange lilies with buds

4 Rust delphiniums

6 bittersweet stems

5 orange daisy stems

3 brown hydrangeas

Autumn leaves

Natural bearded wheat

Other Supplies & Tools:

Sheet moss

Wire cutters

Glue gun and glue

Wooden picks

Floral U-pins

Plastic foam

2 deep orange pillar candles, 2 1/2"
    diameter - one 4" and one 6"

2 plastic candle holders for pillar
    candles

Level of difficulty: Time to complete:

INSTRUCTIONS

1. Trim foam to fit inside bowl. Glue in place.

2. Cut a piece of foam 3" square. Glue and anchor with wood picks at the center back of the bowl. (This gives the candle extra height.)

3. Insert and glue candle holders in foam, placing one on the raised area and one centered at the front left. Place candles in holders.

4. Cover the foam with sheet moss. Secure with floral U-pins.

5. Insert two delphiniums extending to about 12" on the right. Repeat on left side.

6. Wire a wood pick to the grape bunch and insert at the right front cascading over the edge.

7. Insert a cluster of two large pears and one small pear to the left of the grapes.

8. Insert the remaining pears to the left of the taller candle.

9. Using the photo as a guide, insert two lilies and buds behind the grapes and pears at the front of the bowl. Insert one lily and buds to the left of the smaller candle.

10. Fill in around the candles, fruit, and flowers with small clusters of hydrangea and autumn leaves.

11. Add the orange daisies.

12. Insert lengths of bittersweet as desired.

13. Glue small bunches of wheat as shown. ❏

Designer's Tips

• *The flowers in a centerpiece should flow toward the tabletop. If your centerpiece has "airplane wings" shape the flowers to make gentle downward arcs.*

• *If the flowers or fruit seem too bright, mist them with glossy wood-tone spray.*

Round of Blooms

Tall taper candles stretch above the pink and purple blossoms in this easy-to-create design. A plastic foam wreath covered in lush green moss is the container, and the design is simple because you follow the shape of the wreath.

Level of difficulty:

Time to complete:

SUPPLIES

Container:

Plastic foam (Styrofoam®) wreath, 12" diameter

Flowers & Foliage:

3 pink peonies (mass flower)

3 hydrangeas - blue, purple, burgundy (mass flower)

2 purple statice stems (filler flower)

White wax flower (filler flower)

Assorted white and purple filler flowers

Assorted greenery (your choice)

Hot pink star flowers (dried)

Other Supplies & Tools:

Green sheet moss

Floral U-pins

Glue gun and glue

Wire cutters

Floral paddle wire

Wood picks

3 plastic candle holders for tapers

3 taper candles, 15"

1. Pink peony 2. Hydrangea 3. Purple statice
4. White wax flower 5. White filler flower
6. Greenery 7. Hot pink star flower

Instructions begin on page 118.

Photo 1 - Covering the wreath form with moss.

INSTRUCTIONS

1. Cover all but the bottom side of the wreath with green sheet moss. (photo 1) Secure with floral U-pins.

2. Wrap the wreath over the moss with paddle wire to further secure the moss. (photo 2)

3. Place the wreath flat on your work surface. Insert and glue the candle holders at 10 o'clock, 1 o'clock, and 3 o'clock. (photo 3) Insert the candles in the holders.

4. Insert and glue two peonies in front of the 10 o'clock candle. (photo 4) Insert and glue another peony between the other two candles.

5. Attach a cluster of star flowers to a wood pick. (photo 5) Insert behind the 10 o'clock candle. Attach a cluster of star flowers beside the other two candles.

6. Using the photo as a guide, insert and glue hydrangea, wax flowers, statice, additional clusters of star flowers, and/or other filler flowers around each candle. (photo 6) Make sure the flowers follow the curves of the wreath. ❑

Photo 2 - Wrapping the moss with floral wire on a paddle.

Photo 3 - Inserting candle holders in the moss-covered wreath.

Photo 4 - Applying hot glue to the stem of a peony before inserting it.

Designer's Tips

• *Make a centerpiece from a wreath you already have – place the wreath in the center of the table, add some candles, and you'll have a beautiful, easy centerpiece.*

• *Include dried flowers for color. Use them in clusters and attach to a pick for easy insertion.*

• *Be sure to place taper candles at least the distance of two fingers apart on a centerpiece so that as they burn they do not melt each other.*

Photo 5 - Adding a wood pick to a cluster of dried star flowers.

Photo 6 - Inserting a cluster of dried flowers.

Orchid Tray

Orchids remind me of exotic tropical islands; only a few are needed to create a dramatic look. In this arrangement a low tray filled with river pebbles and tea lights holds a few choice orchids. It's a great design for a coffee or dining table.

Level of difficulty:

Time to complete:

SUPPLIES

Container:
Wood or bamboo tray, 12" square

Flowers, Foliage & Accents:
1 phalenopsis orchid stem with foliage
3 lady slipper orchids
1 dendrobium orchid stem
1 curly willow stem
Eucalyptus foliage
String of pearls foliage

Other Supplies & Tools:
Floral foam base material (your choice)
Knife
Glue gun and glue
Reindeer moss
Floral U-pins
River pebbles
5 tea light candles

INSTRUCTIONS

1. Glue a 3" square of floral base material to back left corner of tray.

2. Cover base material with reindeer moss. Glue in place.

3. Fill the remainder of the tray with river pebbles.

4. Position the tea lights at the front right of the tray.

5. Lay the curly willow stem diagonally across the tray and attach it to the base material with glue and floral U-pins.

6. Insert and glue the phalenopsis orchid stem in the center of the base material, curving to the left.

7. Insert three lady slipper orchids on the right side, curving each slightly upward.

8. Insert the dendrobium orchid, centering it in the back left corner.

9. Fill in around the orchids with eucalyptus sprigs and string of pearls.

10. Hide any glue or floral U-pins with glued-on reindeer moss.

Orchid Facts

- *Orchids are the largest plant family on earth, with an estimated 30,000 species. (If you count hybrids, the number jumps to almost 100,000.)*

- *Orchids are found everywhere on the planet except the oceans and Antarctica.*

- *Of all flowers blooming at any one time, one in four is an orchid.*

- *About 90% of orchids live on trees. (This type of plant is called an epiphyte.) About 5% live on rocks (lithophytes). The remaining 5% are rooted in the ground (terrestrials).*

Iris Water Garden

The sparkling clear water, flickering candlelight, and the beautiful shape of iris make
this arrangement special. Although it takes a while to make, the results are worth the effort.

Level of difficulty: �֍ �֍ ✷

Time to Complete:

(The acrylic resin takes about 48 hours to dry.)

SUPPLIES

Container:
10" low clear glass bowl, 8" opening,
  4" tall

Flowers, Foliage & Accents:
4 purple iris
Ivory tallow berry stems
Curly willow
Assorted foliage

Other Supplies & Tools:
12 oz. clear acrylic resin water
Green reindeer moss
Glue gun and glue
Plastic foam (Styrofoam®), 2" square
Wire cutters
Knife
Disposable mixing bowl (a food
  storage container works well)
Wooden spoon
Latex gloves
Newspapers or drop cloth
Paper towels
Soap and water
3 clear votive cups
2 ivory votive candles
40 polished river rocks

INSTRUCTIONS

*The flowers and foliage are added to the design after the acrylic resin is dry; this keeps
the color from bleeding and spoiling the clear water look. Choose a work surface where
the project can remain undisturbed for 48 hours.*

1. Clean the glass bowl, votive cups, and rocks with soap and water. Dry thoroughly.

2. Place the votive cups in a triangular arrangement centered inside the glass bowl.
   Place three rocks inside each votive. Place remaining rocks in the glass bowl,
   spreading them in an even layer.

3. Spread newspapers or a drop cloth on your work surface. Wearing latex gloves,
   mix the acrylic resin according to the package. Stir the mixture thoroughly.

4. Slowly pour the acrylic resin over the rocks. Be sure the votives do not float, and
   adjust rocks as needed. Allow the project to dry undisturbed for 48 hours or
   longer. (How long it takes depends on the temperature and humidity.) Dispose
   of the mixing bowl and clean the spoon and any drips or spills in your work area
   while the resin is still wet. (It is permanent when it dries.)

5. When resin is dry, remove rocks from the votive cups.

6. Trim the foam piece and glue inside one votive cup. Cover the foam with moss.

7. Insert iris in foam with tallest one about 18" in a vertical line.

8. Insert tallow berry stems to the right and left of the iris.

9. Fill in with curly willow and foliage.

10. Place candles in the two remaining votive cups. ❑

Snowflake Reflections

Crisp green pine contrasts beautifully with the icy branches, silver balls, and white pillar candle in this seasonal arrangement. With the matching snowflake votive (instructions below), you'll have a lovely table setting. Place a mirror under the centerpiece and votive for added sparkle.

Level of difficulty:

Time to complete:

SUPPLIES

Container:

Mirrored container, 6" diameter, 4" tall (I used a plastic one.)

Foliage & Accents:

Evergreens (your choice)

Icy branches

2 silver snowflakes, 6" diameter

Silver leaves (your choice)

Other Supplies & Tools:

4 yds. wire-edge sheer silver ribbon, 2-1/2" wide

Small silver ornaments

Glue gun and glue

Scissors

Wire cutters

Knife

Wood picks

Floral wire

Floral foam base material

Plastic pillar candle holder, 3"

White pillar candle, 3" diameter, 9" tall

Optional: Silver glitter spray

INSTRUCTIONS FOR CENTERPIECE

1. Cut foam so it fills about half of the container and is level with opening.
2. Glue foam in back half of container, leaving the front half open. Insert and glue candle holder in foam.
3. Insert stems of pine and evergreen extending on the right and left sides of the container to 10".
4. Insert icy branches on top of evergreens.
5. Fill in around the candle holder with evergreens, leaving the front part of the container open.
6. Insert and glue one snowflake horizontally on the front right and one snowflake on the back left.
7. Cut ribbon in two 2-yd. lengths. Form each length into a bow with 4" loops and 6" streamers. Secure bows at center with floral wire and attach each to a wood pick. Insert one bow to front left and other to back right.
8. Fill opening in container with silver ornaments.
9. Using the photo as a guide, glue silver leaves and silver ornaments around the bows and candle.
10. Place candle in holder.
11. *Option:* Spray arrangement and candle with silver glitter spray. Allow glitter to dry before lighting candle. ❏

Designer's Tip

Have a long banquet table to decorate?
Place two pieces of silver ribbon centered on the length of the table.
Place the centerpiece in the middle on a mirror. Add a snowflake votive near each end of the table on smaller mirrors.

Snowflake Votive

SUPPLIES

1 silver snowflake, 6" diameter

Evergreen

Icy branches

Votive cup and candle

3 silver ornaments

Silver leaf

Poster board, 3" square

INSTRUCTIONS

1. Trim poster board into a circle 2-1/2" in diameter. Glue circle to bottom of snowflake. (This keeps the glue from seeping through when you glue the greenery.)
2. Trim evergreens into small sprigs and glue at top left of snow flake.
3. Glue icy branches and leaves into pine.
4. Glue silver ornaments in place.
5. Place votive cup and candle on the snowflake. ❑

Caring for Arrangements

Proper care will extend the life of your arrangement and keep it fresh looking.
To extend the life of any arrangement, keep it out of direct sun and away from
direct heat and air vents.
Here are some other tips for caring for arrangements:

• **Cleaning silk arrangements.** Most silk arrangements need only an occasional dusting with an artist's brush or feather duster. (A hair dryer on low heat can also remove dust.) Commercial spray cleaners work well on really dusty arrangements; read and follow the manufacturer's instructions.

• **Freshening dried flowers.** Dried flowers can be freshened with a light coating of clear acrylic spray.

• **Storing.** To store an out-of-season arrangement, stuff the bow (if there is one) with tissue paper and place the arrangement in a dark plastic bag. Store in a cool dry place.

• **Reuse and recycle.** If an arrangement has passed its prime, remove the best-looking blossoms, clean them, and use on a wreath.

Metric Conversion Chart

Inches to Millimeters and Centimeters

Inches	MM	CM	Inches	MM	CM
1/8	3	.3	2	51	5.1
1/4	6	.6	3	76	7.6
3/8	10	1.0	4	102	10.2
1/2	13	1.3	5	127	12.7
5/8	16	1.6	6	152	15.2
3/4	19	1.9	7	178	17.8
7/8	22	2.2	8	203	20.3
1	25	2.5	9	229	22.9
1-1/4	32	3.2	10	254	25.4
1-1/2	38	3.8	11	279	27.9
1-3/4	44	4.4	12	305	30.5

Yards to Meters

Yards	Meters
1/8	.11
1/4	.23
3/8	.34
1/2	.46
5/8	.57
3/4	.69
7/8	.80
1	.91
2	1.83
3	2.74
4	3.66
5	4.57
6	5.49
7	6.40
8	7.32
9	8.23
10	9.14

Index

Continued on next page

Index (Continued)